The Joy of UX

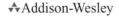

The Joy of UX

User Experience and Interactive Design for Developers

David Platt

✦✦Addison-Wesley

Boston • Columbus • Indianapolis • New York • San Francisco • Amsterdam • Cape Town
Dubai • London • Madrid • Milan • Munich • Paris • Montreal • Toronto • Delhi • Mexico City
São Paulo • Sidney • Hong Kong • Seoul • Singapore • Taipei • Tokyo

Many of the designations used by manufacturers and sellers to distinguish their products are claimed as trademarks. Where those designations appear in this book, and the publisher was aware of a trademark claim, the designations have been printed with initial capital letters or in all capitals.

The author and publisher have taken care in the preparation of this book, but make no expressed or implied warranty of any kind and assume no responsibility for errors or omissions. No liability is assumed for incidental or consequential damages in connection with or arising out of the use of the information or programs contained herein.

For information about buying this title in bulk quantities, or for special sales opportunities (which may include electronic versions; custom cover designs; and content particular to your business, training goals, marketing focus, or branding interests), please contact our corporate sales department at corpsales@pearsoned.com or (800) 382-3419.

For government sales inquiries, please contact governmentsales@pearsoned.com.

For questions about sales outside the U.S., please contact intlcs@pearson.com.

Visit us on the Web: informit.com/aw

Library of Congress Cataloging-in-Publication Data

Names: Platt, David S., author.
Title: The joy of UX : User Experience and interactive design for developers
/ David Platt.
Description: Boston : Addison-Wesley, [2016] | Includes index.
Identifiers: LCCN 2016009039| ISBN 9780134276717 (pbk. : alk. paper) | ISBN
013427671X (pbk. : alk. paper)
Subjects: LCSH: User interfaces (Computer systems) | Human-computer
interaction. | Computer software—Development.
Classification: LCC QA76.9.U83 P54 2016 | DDC 005.4/37—dc23
LC record available at https://lccn.loc.gov/2016009039

ISBN-13: 978-0-13-427671-7
ISBN-10: 0-13-427671-X
Text printed in the United States on recycled paper at RR Donnelley in Crawfordsville, Indiana.
1 16

Publisher
Mark L. Taub

Executive Editor
Laura Lewin

Development Editor
Michael Thurston

Managing Editor
Sandra Schroeder

Full-Service Production Manager
Julie B. Nahil

Copy Editor
Barbara Wood

Indexer
Infodex Indexing Services

Proofreader
Linda Begley

Technical Reviewers
Lars Athle Larsen
Gregg Tompkins
Moshe Raab

Editorial Assistant
Olivia Basegio

Cover Designer
Chuti Prasertsith

Compositor
Shepherd, Inc.

To all my students, from whom I learn so much.

Contents

Foreword

Occasionally you meet a teacher who's so enthusiastic about what he teaches that the enthusiasm rubs off almost contagiously. David is that rare kind of teacher. I've seen it live in his classes and with his students. I see that same love and enthusiasm in *The Joy of UX*, and I know you will too.

I have to confess: I'm the wrong person to write this foreword. I may have the world's worst natural sense of user interface design. But over the years, and especially with the assistance of David Platt, I've produced some pretty great software. The software produced by the teams I've led has generated billions in revenue and has been used by millions of people.

Incredibly, I've also learned to enjoy creating breathtaking UX. I once thought building a great user experience was a tedious process, primarily about colors and fonts and something to do with the golden ratio. Far more critical are the tools and techniques David teaches: empathy for your user, hypothesis testing, and iterating on those hypotheses by watching how users interact with the software. Put another way: fall in love with your users and prioritize their happiness.

When I finally embraced the techniques and processes David writes about in this book, I didn't just end up creating delightful user experiences. It also had a profound effect on how I develop software. At the heart of a great user experience is empathy for the user. Developing this empathy requires a true understanding of who your users are. This changed my entire orientation from thinking about *what* (What code should I write? What language should I use? What is the technology?) to thinking in terms of *who* and *why*. This requires hard work and hard thinking. You must leave your keyboard behind and adventure out into the world. You must meet the people who are using (or will use) your software and talk to them. They will surprise you. They will defy expectations. After you build, you must go back to them and continuously develop your relationship and understanding of how they think, what motivates them, and discover the "why" behind what drives them.

I also learned to take a much more iterative approach to software development. "I should build feature 'X'" turns into a hypothesis that needs to be validated—by the customer. Applying a user-centric process to all feature decisions made my process leaner than just using a Kanban board or Scrum. To determine what to build next, we must determine what will have the highest impact on the user's experience.

These techniques are vital today, especially when building mobile applications. End users have tremendous choices. They are fickle. If they don't grok your application immediately, they'll never touch it again.

You can delight your users by incorporating David's advice into your workflow. Get inside your users' heads, develop a deep understanding and empathy for their lives, test your assumptions, and discover "why."

—Keith Ballinger
Vice President of Product at Xamarin

About the Author

David Platt teaches User Experience Engineering at Harvard University Extension School and at companies all over the world. He's the author of 12 programming books, including *Why Software Sucks* (Addison-Wesley, 2006) and *Introducing Microsoft .NET* (Microsoft Press, 2003). When he finishes working, he spends his free time working some more. When readers ask, "Did you really tape down two of your daughter's fingers so she'd learn how to count in octal?", he just smiles. Microsoft named him a Software Legend in 2002. Dave lives in Ipswich, Massachusetts. You can contact him at www.joyofux.com.

UX RULES THE ROOST

User experience (UX) is the primary driver of competitive advantage in software today. Programs with bad UX just won't sell, nor will the hardware or services they are supposed to enable.

Good UX is not that hard, but it requires you to think in new ways. This book shows you how, step by step, with examples along the way.

Your Biggest Advantage

UX is the primary driver of competitive advantage in the software industry today. Whether you design and sell software as a product (Microsoft), or use it to sell hardware (Apple) or services (UPS), the user experience of your software is absolutely critical.

Just as smoking in public places was once common, it was once common to force users to contort themselves into five-dimensional hyper-pretzels to match their software—to become "computer literate," in the term of that day. UX guru Alan Cooper wrote that a computer-literate user is one who "has been hurt so often that the scar tissue is so thick that he no longer feels the pain." Users once accepted this as the price of getting their computing jobs done. They won't do that anymore.

Remember when Apple was left for dead in 1997, kept alive solely by a cash infusion from Microsoft so that Microsoft could claim it wasn't a monopoly? How did Apple become the most valuable company ever seen on the face of the planet? By turning out great UX, for which its customers pay premium prices. That's how important UX has become.

UX is critical to the enterprise sector as well. In December of 2014, Avon had to kill a new version of its order management software. The *Wall Street Journal* reported that the company's sales force of independent reps "found the new system so burdensome and disruptive to their daily routine that many left Avon."

Even IBM, the stodgiest of stodgy companies, recently announced that it was spending $100 million on its UX consulting business, opening ten new labs worldwide and hiring 1,000 new workers.

Whatever you are doing, and whomever you are doing it for, you need an excellent UX. It's not optional anymore.

UX Is *Not* Fonts and Colors

Too many developers and managers think that UX design is selecting colors and fonts and button radii. Nothing could be further from the truth. The rounded window corners and cutesy animations are the last and least important pieces of the UX. My fellow Software Legend Billy Hollis calls that stuff "decoration, not design."

What's the difference between user experience (UX) and user interface (UI)? As is always the case when specific meanings are forced onto generic words, it is difficult to find any two writers who agree on what they mean. Throughout this book, I will use UI to mean the decoration function that is the very last thing you do to a piece of software. I will use UX in the meaning published by Jakob Nielsen and Donald Norman, who wrote that "user experience encompasses all aspects of the end-user's interaction with the company, its services, and its products." That means that anything the user ever sees, hears, touches, or thinks about is the UX: a program's workflows, its feature sets, its required inputs, the form of its outputs.

Figure 0.1 illustrates the differences. Figure 0.1a shows a product. Consider this to be the computing job that you need done. Figure 0.1b shows the UI, the tool with which you interact with that product. Figure 0.1c shows the full UX, the totality of your interaction with that product.

The battle for good UX is usually won or lost long before the program reaches the decorators. Think of your program as a piece of furniture—say, a table. The decoration is the surface finish on that table. Certainly tables should be finished well rather than poorly, and so should your programs. But if you build the table out of the wrong material, one that doesn't satisfy the user's needs, even the best finish in the world can't help. If your user wants a decorative table for a nature-inspired living room, choosing wood will probably make him happy. On the other hand, if your user needs a working table for a cafeteria kitchen that undergoes daily sanitizing, metal would be far better. And backing up a step, does your user really need a table, or would a chair solve his problem better?

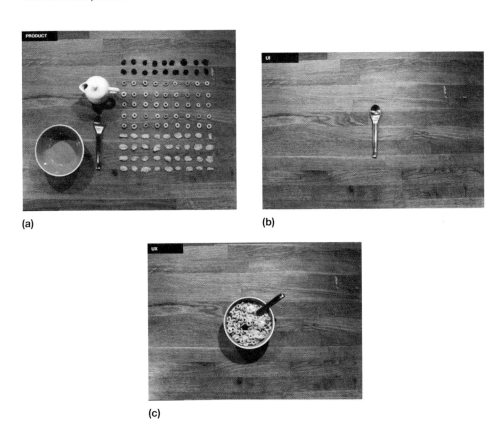

(a)   (b)

(c)

Figure 0.1   (a) Product, (b) UI, and (c) UX. (Ed Lea, Product Design)

Fundamental Example

Let's look at an example of the fundamental development decisions that make or break a UX. I was teaching in Sweden some time ago and opened up Google by using its base address, www.google.com. Its servers detected the country in which I was located and automatically replied with the Swedish version of the page (Figure 0.2). This decision is correct for most users most of the time and requires just one click (lower center) to fix it permanently (persistent cookie) if it's ever wrong.

On the other hand, consider UPS.com, home of the package delivery company (Figure 0.3). UPS.com requires users to select their country before they can do anything at all. That takes 30 clicks if you're in Sweden. You also have to explicitly tell the site to remember you (see the check box) or it'll make you do it again next time. That's no way to treat customers.

What happened here? Were the Google programmers so much smarter than the UPS programmers that Google could detect the incoming country of a Web request while UPS couldn't?

No way. According to UPS.com, its site handled over 100 million tracking requests on its peak day in 2014. The UPS programmers have to be pretty good to build a site that successfully handles such a large volume. There's no way that such skillful programmers wouldn't know how to find the IP address of an incoming request, and hence determine its probable country of origin. (It's not difficult: simple static table lookup, cache it in RAM for speed, update the table once per day. Easy.) UPS is therefore choosing to make users explicitly enter their country, instead of automatically detecting it.

Figure 0.2   Google home page accessed from Sweden.

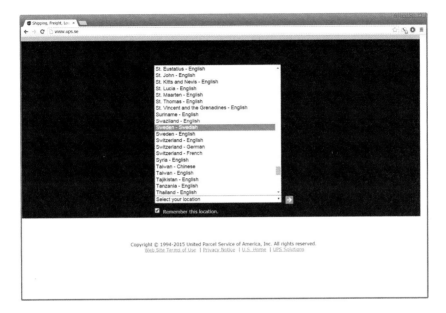

Figure 0.3 UPS home page accessed from Sweden.

In my opinion, UPS is committing *the* cardinal sin of all UX work: failing to put itself in its users' shoes. The technologists who made this choice are behaving like the geeks they undoubtedly are (and I am, and you are too). We are trained mathematically, logically. We get it hammered into us from middle-school algebra onward: a theorem that's true in 99 cases but false in the 100th case is a false theorem. Bad geek. Throw it away; go find a true one. UPS won't make a guess because it might be wrong.

That's acceptable for mathematical theorems, but not for human users. Unlike a theorem, if your program makes 99 out of 100 users happy, you are probably having a pretty good day. And it's probably more important to make those 99 users happy again tomorrow than it is to figure out how to please that 100th user—especially if what that user wants would annoy the other 99. Clearly there are cases when that's not good enough—air traffic control springs to mind. But for most business and consumer situations, the world is a better place when you handle the main case seamlessly and fix unusual cases only as they arise, rather than annoying all users by making them do work that the site could be and should be doing on their behalf.

Google's language selection algorithm doesn't always guess right; maybe the request isn't actually coming from Sweden, maybe It Is but the user doesn't speak Swedish (me), or maybe it is and the user does speak Swedish but doesn't want to right now (for example, a Swedish college student practicing English). But making its best guess, and having the user correct any resulting errors, is a large net profit for the overall user population. Which company's approach makes you feel that it values your time and effort, and makes you want to come back? In fact,

Google has thought so long and hard about its users that it has figured out how to recognize a UPS tracking number. If you type one directly into Google search, Google will offer to track it for you (Figure 0.4). If you click that link, Google will jump you straight to the UPS tracking page (Figure 0.5) with the correct language already selected. That's why I always use Google to track my UPS packages, instead of hassling with UPS.com. And I can't suppress an ironic chuckle as I do so.

You can see that this isn't a *graphical* design problem, not at all. Both sites have their logos, their corporate color palettes and fonts, everything. But one site makes all users do extraneous work—overhead, excise, distraction—before users can even begin to do what they went to the site for: their business logic, in this case tracking packages. The other site jumps right in and starts banging away as best it can, taking care of most users seamlessly and allowing corrections as needed.

The difference between these sites is one of *interaction design*, sometimes known as behavioral design, and occasionally as information architecture. That's what this book is about. We won't be discussing graphical design. We won't be discussing how to program these designs, either. There are lots of books on both of these topics. We'll be studying *how to decide what should get programmed*. And we will always, *always*, be hammering on the side of the user.

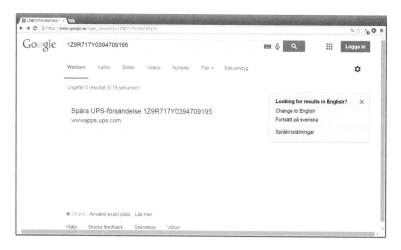

Figure 0.4 Google automatically recognizes a UPS tracking number and offers to track the package.

Figure 0.5 Google automatically displays the UPS tracking page in the language of the user's browser—much easier than going through UPS.com.

PLATT'S FIRST, LAST, AND ONLY LAW OF UX DESIGN

The Talmud speaks of the impatient man who came to the famous rabbi Hillel, saying, "Teach me the Torah [the first five books of the Hebrew Bible] while I stand on one foot." Hillel replied, "What you do not want done to yourself, do not do to others. The rest is commentary, go and study."

Do you want to know everything there is to know about UX? I can answer in one sentence, Platt's First, Last, and Only Law of User Experience:

KNOW THY USER, FOR HE IS NOT THEE.

The rest is commentary, my friends. Come and study along with me.

The Three Fundamental Corollaries

I majored in physics as an undergraduate, and there's still enough of the physicist in me to insist on setting forth the fundamental principles from which I derive my judgments as to good and bad usage. Starting from the FLaO Law mentioned in the sidebar, we can derive the following corollaries:

- **First Corollary:** The software that you write has zero value in and of itself. The only value that your software ever has or ever will have is the degree to which it makes your users happier or more productive.

- **Second Corollary:** The software increases the happiness or productivity of users in one of two ways. First, it could help a user solve a specific problem—write an article, pay a bill, navigate a car. Or it might put the user into a state that she finds pleasurable—listening to music, playing a game, video phoning her grandchildren. Those are the only two cases that ever can exist, though sometimes they blend into a hybrid.

- **Third Corollary:** In neither of these cases do users want to think about the programs they are using. At all. Ever. In the former case, they want to think about the problem they are solving: the wording of the document they are writing, or whether they have enough money to pay their bills, and which unpaid creditor would hurt them the most. In the latter case, the users want to get into that pleasurable state as quickly as they can and stay there as long as they can. Anything that delays the start of their fix, or distracts them from it while they're enjoying it, is even less welcome than the interruption of a work task.

To summarize these three corollaries: Users don't care about your program, or you either. Never have, never will. Your mother might, because you wrote it and she loves you, and then again she might not; but no one else does. Users care only about their own productivity or their own pleasure. Every single user of every single program wants what Donald Norman calls the "invisible computer" in his landmark book of that title.

You can see in that earlier simple example that Google does its best to be as invisible as it can, while UPS does not. With the FLaO Law and its corollaries in mind, let's examine another common case.

Example: Save Me?

Here's a situation you see every day. It's probably become second nature, to the point where you don't think about it anymore. But we're going to think about it now.

You open a document in Microsoft Word. You add or edit some text, and then you go to close Word. What does Word do? It pops up a dialog box asking, "Do you want to save changes?" (Figure 0.6). The beret-wearing, incense-burning graphical designer can decorate the "Save Changes?" dialog box with nifty fonts and color gradients and nicely rounded corners. But he doesn't, can't, address the question of whether the program should prompt the user on exit, as it does, or whether it should automatically save changes as they are made, as does Microsoft OneNote. Which would make the user happier and more productive? It falls to us, the UX interaction designers, to make that determination. What should we choose?

Start by doing the arithmetic. Word requires a choice and a mouse click each time the user closes a document. If the user has 100 editing sessions, he makes 100 choices, 100 clicks. If we switch to automatic saving, we have to put the capability of a complete rollback somewhere

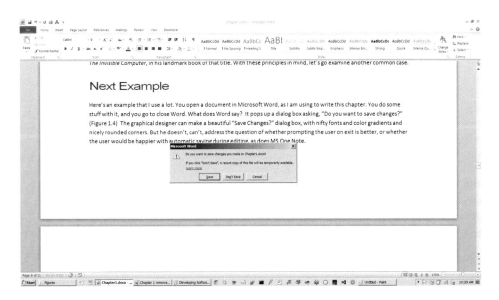

Figure 0.6 Microsoft Word, prompting the user to save changes. Why not save automatically, as does Microsoft OneNote?

else—possibly a "Discard Entire Session" item on the Edit menu, which would take perhaps five clicks to access. If users save their changes 99% of the time, automatic saving would eliminate 95 clicks out of every 100 in the saving process, a huge reduction of overall user effort.[1] If users save their changes only 50% of the time, automatic saving would actually increase the overall user effort by a lot; every 100 clicks in the saving process now mushroom to 250 clicks.[2] Which choice is right for your program?

As usual, it depends. How often do you save your changes in Word? Or look at it the other way: how often do you screw up your document so badly that you discard the changes by selecting "Don't Save"?

Wrong question. Are you developing this app for yourself? Almost certainly not. Then what does it matter what you yourself do? It doesn't. Not in the slightest. Read the FLaO Law again: Thy user is not thee.

How often do *your users* save their changes, versus how often do *they* discard their changes? Entirely different question. Still, don't you feel yourself wanting to say, "Well, I hardly ever see them discarding"? Again, those are your own preferences talking. It is surprisingly difficult to

---

1. The 99 users who save changes go from one click to zero. The one guy who wants to discard all his changes now goes from one click to five clicks. One hundred clicks now shrink to only five.
2. The 50 users who save changes go from one click to zero. The other 50 guys who discard all their changes go from one click to five clicks. One hundred clicks now mushroom to 250.

remove yourself from this equation. You subconsciously resist the notion that your users are different from yourself. So what do you do?

You could try asking the actual users, if you can find them. If you work on an in-house development team, building programs for use inside your company, this could work well. You go to the floor where the users are and ask them. However, there are snags with this approach. Are the users willing to talk to you? Can they remember accurately? Are they afraid of looking stupid? Will their bosses allow them to take the time? Talking to actual users is a very good start. Chapters 1 and 3 discuss ways of obtaining information from this channel. But you can't always get it.

If you don't work on an in-house development team, that is, if you build products for external customers, the problem gets harder. Suppose you asked people in your office. Your coworkers, by definition, spend all day, every day, developing software for sale. Do they resemble your user population? Unless you are in the business of building software development tools, probably not. Whatever they would tell you is probably misleading for your user population. Microsoft has stumbled over this problem more than once.

So how do you find out what percentage of users save their changes? Not by some mystical telepathic intuition, known only to crystal gazers who burn incense and eat sprouts and wear berets, but by collecting hard engineering data via telemetry, over many more users than you could afford to test in the lab. Chapter 5 explains telemetry in more detail. You could also do some early usability lab testing, as described in Chapter 4.

Bake UX In from the Beginning

The biggest single mistake that I see companies making is not starting their UX planning at the beginning of a project. "We need to get the services in place first; then we'll think about what it looks like." That's crazy. That's like saying to an architect who is designing a house, "We won't ask who's going to live here until we get the heating and the plumbing in place." Are you building a house for a downsizing older couple? You'll want a full bath on the ground floor with a wide door and the potential for grab bars. For a younger couple with two kids and planning four more? Entirely different problem. The last thing you want to do is to spend your development budget before you know even the most basic things about what you're building. And the UX determines that.

As you can see from the previous examples, UX design decisions determine the code that needs to be written, not just in the top layers that handle the user interactions, but reaching down to the lowest levels of the application. In the case of Word, the structure of the entire Undo mechanism depends on UX design decisions about when and how files get saved. And in the Google versus UPS case earlier in this chapter, the developers who build the home page need to know if the information about the user's country will be available to them when their code runs (Google), or if they need to get that information from the users and put it somewhere for rest of the site's code to use (UPS).

Good UX design starts at the very beginning of a project. It's not a superficial layer. It permeates all levels of an application, as character and honor (or lack thereof) do a human personality. And it needs attention through all stages of program development, nay, throughout all stages of the program life cycle, as character and honor need attention throughout all stages of the human life cycle.

Clients sometimes ask me to critique their UXs just before they ship. That's way too late to change anything. The architecture is set, the budgets spent, the attitudes hardened. Consider yourself warned.

Why Developers Don't Consider UX

A computer that users can't figure out how to use, or that requires expensive training to use, or that makes expensive mistakes because the program misleads users, is a very expensive paper-weight. Yet many developers or architects think they don't need to understand UX. Here's why they say that, and why they're wrong.

Our Projects Are Low-Level, So UX Doesn't Matter

Nonsense. Every project has some connection to a human user somewhere. Even a programmatic Web service needs error reporting, installation and configuration, status- and performance-monitoring dashboards, and so on. If a project has only small amounts of UX, that's all the more reason that those pieces need to work well. Twenty years ago, you might have gotten away with a dialog box saying, "Web Service Failure, Error 20. Consult Documentation." Today you would get laughed out of the arena for shipping something like that.

Marketing Decides Our UX

It's wise to have a good relationship with your marketing department. They certainly feel pain points from the customer and bring them back to you. At the same time, marketeers are not interaction designers. They might give you the first clue as to what would make the customer happier and more productive—"Customers complain that they're losing work when our app crashes"—but it's up to you to take it from there. How often does it happen? How do you detect and measure it? To fix it: Auto-save? Rollback? How often? Configurable? Imagine asking these questions of your marketing department, and tell me if they're really driving the UX. They're not; you are, even if they sound the initial alarm.

You should also be talking to your tech support department. They feel your customers' pain far more immediately and brutally than the glad-handing marketeers.

We Have a UX Group That Does That Stuff

Some large companies have a UX design group that approves every user interaction. If you have one of these, you've already found that their time is in tight supply, as it is for other ultra-specialists such as ophthalmologists. You can get a 15-minute appointment in six months if you beg. They can't follow up or help you iterate. You need to understand what they tell you in your far-too-limited interactions and implement those principles day to day to make the best use of the thimblefuls of their concentrated wisdom that you actually get.

Also, their time is (quite rationally) dedicated to your company's primary, outward-facing programs. They don't have time for internal or second-tier apps. A company that has this type of group values good UX. The apps you work on are held to a higher standard. But your bosses don't give you the skill set or resources to meet these demands, now do they? You have to be ready to do the day-to-day work at a project team level.

UX Is for the Beret-Heads

Also known as graphical designers, more accurately they are decorators. As we've seen, the UX game is almost always won or lost before it reaches them. Be nice to them. But the main battle isn't theirs, it's ours.

Where to Get the Skills

Precisely because your UX needs attention throughout the development process, you need someone with UX skills assigned directly to your design team. This person will know that the correct choice in the document-saving example comes not from arguing personal tastes and philosophies, but from hard user data—knowing what percentage of documents are discarded rather than saved. And she will know how to obtain that data, ideally by instrumenting the program, but through skillful interviews and observations if that can't be done. Where are we going to get such people, and how are we going to manage them?

Regular programmer geeks don't know how to do it; they mistakenly think that their users resemble their geeky selves, and their UX designs come out looking like Visual Studio. Sometimes marketing people want to get into the act, figuring that they interact with customers so they know what they need. That's like saying that you have teeth in your mouth, so you know how to do a root canal. Graphic designers sometimes try to get into the picture, but as you can see, this interaction design isn't fundamentally a graphical problem. How do we get the people we need?

Consider the US Army, specifically its most basic unit of operations, the infantry platoon. It consists of a green second lieutenant in nominal command, an experienced first sergeant who's really running it, and about 40 fighters. And each platoon has a medic. The medic is not a fully qualified doctor, although the platoon soldiers customarily address him as "Doc." The army can't afford to create enough full-fledged doctors to place one in each platoon. The medic is trained in battlefield first intervention to stabilize the wounded soldier—stopping severe bleeding, starting IVs, opening airways, and so on. Having this intervention immediately available is the first link in the amazing chain of battlefield casualty survival today.

What we need in the UX business is the equivalent of a medic. We need someone who knows the basic concepts of UX design and their most common applications—for example, knowing that data is the key to most UX questions, and knowing how to start obtaining it. Someone who knows how to generate a user persona quickly and accurately, to help the design team grasp the slippery concept of "the user." Someone who knows how to do a usability test quickly and cheaply so it doesn't hold up the project, or get skipped to keep it from holding up the project. The key point is getting UX questions answered quickly. As in trauma medicine, getting treated in the golden hour is key.

Sometimes you get pushback on the medic concept in companies that recognize the importance of UX and have a central UX team that wants to control everything. Continuing the army medic analogy, these are the highly skilled surgeons in the base hospital. If you frame it right, these people will be the biggest beneficiaries of having UX medics on the project teams, for example, having the first round of usability tests already done when they get called in to evaluate the puzzling data.

You Can Do This

My readers and students tell me that the hardest part of producing a good UX is knowing where to start. It is so very tempting to jump right into the development—OK, we've got this project, the schedule is tight (it's always tight), let's get going. No, don't waste time on that persona nonsense, we have to get going. Stories? What are they? Never mind, fire up Visual Studio (or Expression Blend if you're less geeky). Jump right in and drag and drop. Should we have check boxes here? Radio buttons? How about a set of tabs instead?

I recall the opening of *The Joy of Cooking*, one of the *Joy* books that inspired my title choice for this volume. Written for the person who knew nothing about cooking, it began with the instruction "Stand facing the stove." That's how I've written this book, starting you from zero.

After this introduction, each of the first seven chapters represents one step to a great UX. (That's five steps fewer than it takes to kick the booze.) Each chapter introduces one specific UX design technique. I've placed them in the order in which I generally use them in my practice, though as you'll see, there are certain loopbacks and iterations. If you follow these steps, without skipping any, you will come up with something good, or at least a whole lot better than if you had just jumped in and flailed away. With my usual modesty, I call them the Platt UX Protocol.

Chapter 8 and Chapter 9 each presents a case study, working the seven steps from beginning to end on a specific project. I present personas, stories, sketches, testing, telemetry, security, and final simplification. My students tell me that this, the end-to-end discussion about how all the pieces fit together, is their favorite part of the class.

Here's what each chapter deals with:

- **Chapter 1: Personas**—We learn and understand who the user actually is. Is the user male or female? Old or young? High or low disposable income? Education type and level? What do users hope for and what do they fear? We write up this data in the form of a persona, an artificial person who represents our user population.

- **Chapter 2: What Do Users Want? (And Where, and When, and Why?)**—We work on understanding a user's motives and activities in using our software. What problem is the user trying to solve, or what pleasurable state does the user want to maintain? What would the user consider to be the characteristics of a good solution or pleasurable state? We represent this information through stories, narratives written from the user's point of view. (If you're familiar with stories as part of agile development, you'll see that these are different.)

- **Chapter 3: Sketching and Prototyping**—We know who the users are and what they need. Now, and only now, do we start sketching out some possible solutions. Using a low-fidelity editor (in this book, Balsamiq), we generate mockups quickly, so that we can begin the iteration process of testing them and refining them.

- **Chapter 4: Testing on Live Users**—We have some mockups illustrating possible solutions. Now we test them, ideally on actual users but on user surrogates or representatives if that's not possible. The degree of fidelity that we show to the users depends on the progress of our project. We will generally iterate steps 3 and 4 several times during the course of the project.

- **Chapter 5: Telemetry and Analytics**—We plan for our applications to have some sort of telemetry, so that we can understand what users are actually doing with it. We will see which features they are using, and in what order, as well as information about their hardware. Failing to provide telemetry in today's environment would be like practicing medicine without X-rays or lab tests.

- **Chapter 6: Security and Privacy**—Security and usability are often seen as polar opposites. In this chapter, we carefully examine the interaction between these two and understand what happens when it breaks. We work out a plan for securing our application as tightly as needed, while still making it as usable as possible.

- **Chapter 7: Making It Just Work**—As we get closer to release, we start looking not to add features, but for ways to remove user effort from the features we have. This is the level of final polish that we give our program.

- **Chapter 8: Case Study: Commuter Rail Mobile App**—We work through all of the steps as we design a new mobile app for Boston's commuter rail system.
- **Chapter 9: Case Study: Medical Patient Portal**—We work through all of the steps as we design a new Web portal for a Boston-area hospital system.

This Book's Web Site

This book, like everything else in the world, has its own Web site, JoyOfUX.com. Figure 0.7 shows a screenshot.

You can find on it all of the resources to which I refer in this book, such as persona templates. I will also be adding case studies, similar to the ones at the end of this book. So come back every month or so and have a look at them. And if you have a case study that you'd like to contribute, I'd be happy to see it.

And Here We Go . . .

To paraphrase Arlo Guthrie's song about resisting the Vietnam War draft: If one guy does it, they'll think he's crazy. And if three guys do it, they'll think it's an organization. And if fifty people do it, they'll think it's a movement.

And that's what I hope our revolt against bad UX will become. So let's get to it.

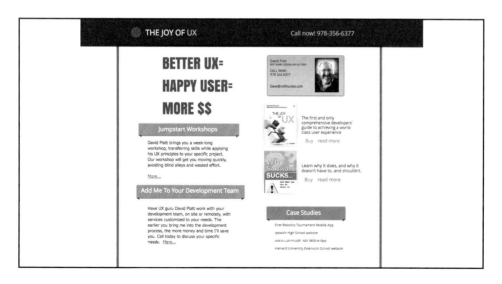

Figure 0.7   JoyOfUx.com Web site.

CHAPTER 1

PERSONAS

The bedrock principle of all user experience design is understanding who the users of this particular app really are—not who you wish they were or hope they'll somehow morph into. Without this knowledge, the UX always gets designed for a user who resembles the developer, which the real users are guaranteed to hate.

It is, however, extremely difficult to grasp the concept of "the user." That nebulous term wriggles and twists as you try to apply it to specific situations. We need to understand and represent the users of our program in a way that our minds can grasp and absorb. In this chapter, we learn to construct an artificial user called a *persona*, which makes the user population real to us.

Putting a Face on the User

Humans are not good at grasping generalities. Our brains evolved for living in small tribes. We are constructed to care about specific individuals, not abstract masses.

The charity Save the Children figured this out in its marketing years ago: "You can save Maria Pastora for $16 a month. Or you can turn the page." So did Stalin, with his (probably misattributed) quote: "A single death is a tragedy; a million deaths is a statistic." When we start designing computer programs, we find that our brains can grasp and understand a specific person far more easily and clearly than the nebulous concept of "the user."

Let's prove this with an experiment. Ask yourself, "Is the user going to like this feature?" Now do the same with a specific person: "Is Aunt Millie going to like this feature?" You can feel different parts of your brain lighting up as you contemplate the specific person rather than the vague concept.

If that example doesn't grab you, try this one. When my daughter started using Facebook, I warned her that if she didn't carefully lock down her account, anyone in the world could see what she posted there. For my caring wisdom, I got an eye roll and a roar that I can't transliterate. Seeing that the generality had no effect, I tried a specific example: if she didn't lock things down tighter than a gnat's ass, *I* would be able to see everything that she posted there. *That* got her attention, and she locked her account down very tightly indeed.

To make our user population understandable to designers and developers, we paradoxically need to boil it down to a specific individual who embodies the characteristics of our group. We do this by creating an artificial person. We call such a construct a *persona*, from the Latin word for "mask."

We will then conduct all design discussions in terms of this persona. We will not ask, "Should our app show the time in local or UTC?" or even "Which would the user understand better, local or UTC?" Instead we will use the persona: "Who is in charge of billing? Eva is. Is Eva thinking in terms of local time or UTC? Does Eva even know how to *spell* UTC? I think Eva would be a whole lot happier with local time." Again, note the differences in your thoughts as you consider the nebulous case of "the user" as opposed to the specific person, even though the latter is fictional.

Creating the Simplest Persona

We can create a simple persona very easily. It won't take us more than a day, tops. It will convey a surprising amount of information on its own. It will also provide a foundation to which we will add other descriptive items, to make the persona even richer.

Figure 1.1 shows a persona for a genealogy (family tree) app that I worked on once. (I've placed this persona and the Microsoft Word template into this book's downloadable resources for your benefit.)

I always like to start my personas by choosing a name. The name converts the persona from a stranger into someone you know. The first thing you give a new baby is a name; "the baby" doesn't cut it for long, does it? In addition to being a handle for the person, the name communicates a great deal of information to your subconscious mind, for example, ethnicity (Sunil, Maria, Guðrun). More subtly, it places your user in an age bracket: Mary was the most popular name for girls in the United States through about the 1960s, so you will tend to picture anyone named Mary as middle-aged or older. A name also sets the formality of the relationship you want to have with the persona: William Jefferson Blythe III versus Bill Clinton. I've given this persona the name Aunt Millie. Ah, feel her settling into your mind.

Aunt Millie	"I want to get all of this down for my grandchildren, while I'm still here and have most of my marbles."

Genealogy App Usage Info
Parents' generation still living: mother in nursing home
Siblings: 3
Children: 3
Grandchildren: 5

Hardware/Software
PC: Dell 2 GHz Pentium single core 1 gig RAM 200 GB hard drive 1024x768 VGA, Windows XP
Phone: POTS (plain old telephone service), clamshell phone, doesn't text
Tablet: doesn't have one

Personal Information
Age: 68
Sex: F
Education: East Overshoe NJ High School '64, secretarial curriculum, a few community college courses, but no degree
Car: 2006 Ford Escort
Drink: Vendange Chardonnay, $7.00 for a 1.5 liter bottle
Hobby: Sewing

Character Cues
Pet Peeve: "When the computer does all that stuff that it shouldn't do."
Friends Say: "A little spacy. Talks best early in the day. Really proud of her grandchildren."

Figure 1.1   Genealogy app persona.

The genealogy program for which she represents the user population deals with the tracking of family relationships. The title "Aunt" starts you thinking along family lines and also suggests someone a generation older than you. The diminutive name "Millie" suggests informality and also reinforces the suggestion of her relative age. The name "Mildred" peaked in popularity around 1920. You don't see many Millies walking around today, and any thoughts you have of them will tend to be of older ladies. "Aunt Jennifer" or "Aunt Ashley" suggests a completely different person. See how even the first two words of the persona are communicating with your subconscious mind?

Your persona needs a picture. Your subconscious mind absorbs an enormous amount of information visually via the right side of your brain. Geeks often omit the picture, because they're left-brain kinds of people. But a persona won't work if you do that.

Figure 1.2 shows some of the pictures that I've used in personas. Notice how much they communicate: the geeky software architect sketching out the system, the puzzled manager who's in way over his head but unable to retire because his pension isn't vested, that nasty office accountant who denied reimbursement for your $5 airport cappuccino because you lost the receipt. I don't have to label them, do I? You know from the pictures who I'm talking about. Aunt Millie's picture shows an older lady, grandmotherly, smiling nicely—someone you want to help.

When you create personas to represent the users of mobile apps, you will find that the picture also helps you grasp the context in which that app will be used. Where are the users going to be? What's going on around them? Who else is in the environment? That's critical for mobile apps in a way that it isn't for desktop apps. Figure 1.3 shows some examples.

You can get pictures in many places on the Web. I usually start with iStockPhoto.com. That site has a lot of good pictures for low prices, $10 to $20 apiece, and a decent search engine. Don't

Figure 1.2 Example persona photos. (Photos © iStock.com/-MG-, junial, and DRB Images, LLC)

Figure 1.3   Example persona photos for mobile device apps. (Photos © iStock.com/Susan Chiang, FredFroese, and Anna Bryukhanova)

use a photo that you stole that contains a watermark. It looks like hell and you look like a crook, a lazy crook at that. Buy it fair and square, as I (mostly) do.

After the name and picture comes the tagline. This is a short, memorable phrase that sums up the persona in as few words as possible. It's sort of like a slogan, but more explanatory if possible. "Failure is not an option" is a classic. Aunt Millie expresses herself by saying, "I want to get all of this down for my grandchildren, while I'm still here and have most of my marbles."

You can tell when you get this basic persona right. Look at Figure 1.4. The picture is world-shaking. The guy's tagline is a little long, at 54 words, but I let him have that much space because he uses it so well. The name is the only one he could possibly have. Do you have the slightest doubt just what kind of a person this particular user is? Can't you just predict what he'd like and what he'd hate, what sort of software would work for him (had he lived to become a user of software)? Sure you can. The picture, the name, and the tagline all work together, and it's a beautiful thing.

Winston

"You ask, what is our policy? I will say: It is to wage war, by sea, land and air, with all our might and with all the strength that God can give us; to wage war against a monstrous tyranny, never surpassed in the dark, lamentable catalogue of human crime. That is our policy."

Figure 1.4   Name, photo, and tagline working together beautifully.

Adding Detail

The name, picture, and tagline are the bedrock on which we build a persona. Even this small example shows you how effective they are. But we need to add more items to make the persona really sing. It's time to start fleshing out those details. The following sections explain the other items we'll use.

The Big Three Details

The three most important details are age, gender, and education level. Men and women experience and use technology in entirely different ways. As retailing guru Paco Underhill discussed in his book *Why We Buy: The Science of Shopping* (Simon & Schuster, 2008), "Men are in love with the technology itself, with the gee-whiz factor, with the horsepower. . . . [They're] gathered around the barbecue comparing the size of their hard drives and the speed of their modems. As they say, it's a dude thing." Women, on the other hand, "take a completely different approach to the world of high-tech. They take technologies and turn them into appliances. They strip even the fanciest gizmo of all that is mysterious and jargony in order to determine its usefulness. Women look at technology and see its purpose, its reason—what it can do [for them]. The promise of technology is always that it will make our lives easier and more efficient. Women are the ones who demand that it fulfill its purpose." You probably knew the user's gender when you chose the name and the picture, but it's critical that you get it right, so stop now and make sure that your data on user gender really is good.

I asked the client who built the genealogy application mentioned earlier what his user demographics were. He told me that his user population was 75% female. That's why I chose Aunt Millie instead of Uncle Henry for the persona.

Age is also key to understanding your user population. Almost all programmers and designers are young, since this profession hasn't been around as long as, say, masonry. They do not automatically understand what their older users need. Older users tend to have worse vision and less precise hand movement. They are not as quick to understand new things. They don't multitask as well, and they find excess motion confusing. And they tend to have older, less powerful hardware—often their adult children's castoffs, with tech support provided by their grandchildren.

The user's age also indicates how long computing has been part of his life. At my parents' retirement community, all official communication is still done on paper—the menus, the activity schedules, the party announcements; everything. That age cohort didn't get their first computers until their fifties or sixties, so they never got really comfortable with digital technology. On the other hand, if you're looking to reach today's college students, you can reach them only on their smartphones. A Windows PC is something that their parents use for boring stuff like balancing checkbooks.

My genealogy app client told me that 85% of his users were 50 years or older, and 40% were age 70 or older. I guess younger people are more interested in finding a partner with whom to create descendants than they are in writing down their ancestors. I placed Aunt Millie just around the app's median of 68.

Finally we come to educational level. Developers all have college degrees. Twenty years ago, most users also had college degrees, but today four out of five do not. You need to know what type of educational level to expect in your user population. An app aimed at college grads will not appeal to high school dropouts, and vice versa. Aunt Millie's high school education, with the secretarial curriculum, is a little bit lower than my client's customer base. I wanted to make sure that the developers didn't assume too much on her part.

Business Interaction

The persona needs to contain some sort of information about how the user relates to our app's business operations. This will obviously vary from one business domain to another. If we were writing an app for airline pilots, we might include something about how frequently they fly and how long each flight is. If we were designing instead a medical app for use by a patient, we might put in her diagnosis and treatment to date.

For Aunt Millie, I included some information about her genealogy, the number of relatives she has in each generation.

Hardware and Software

It is important to know the kind of hardware and software with which the persona will be running our app. Does he spend time and money to have the latest devices? Or exactly the opposite? Perhaps somewhere in between? Not only is this technical information important on its own, but it also indicates the users' feelings about their technology. A user who always buys the latest iPhone will have a completely different relationship with his gear than someone who owns a Dell desktop and upgrades reluctantly and seldom. Each will expect, treasure, tolerate, or reject completely different approaches to the program's interaction.

Aunt Millie, typical for users of her age, has an old Windows XP PC. She doesn't see any reason to upgrade. It does what she needs it to do, and she wouldn't want to spend money improving it. If one of her kids offered her a Windows 7 PC, she might take it. Then again, she has this one set up the way she wants it, so maybe not. No way, nohow would she want the tiles of Windows 8 or 10. And constantly raising her arm to touch the monitor would be hell on her arthritis, so no touchscreen. Windows XP will probably outlast her.

Grokkability Items

We now have the key information that a persona needs, and it is tempting to stop at this point. But adding certain kinds of information will make us say, "Oh, yeah, I know this guy."

I call this "grokkability," from the verb "to grok" in Robert Heinlein's *Stranger in a Strange Land*. He defines *grok* as "to understand so thoroughly that the observer becomes a part of the observed. . . ." That's what we want our persona to help us do with our users.

The grokkability items can be anything that makes sense to you, whichever receptor site your brain finds itself binding to. Following is a selection of some of the things that I've seen over the years. Don't pick too many, perhaps three or four, and don't spend too long on them. It's spice, not substance.

■ Car	■ Goals	■ Movie favorites
■ Cell phone	■ Hobbies	■ Political views
■ Drink	■ Hopes	■ Religion
■ Exercise	■ Last book read	■ Restaurant
■ Family members	■ Music player	■ Tablet
■ Fears	■ Music taste	■ TV programs

For Aunt Millie, I put in details about her car, which makes her seem sensible and boring and not especially wealthy. I gave her a hobby, sewing, which reinforces her age and gender cohort. And I gave her a preferred drink of inexpensive wine, suggesting that she's frugal and not all that interested in "the finer things in life."

Personality Cues

I've had good success with two other items that don't appear in other works on personas. I find that these personality cues give me insight from a different axis, which I find very useful.

The first is the notion of what other people think about the persona. As Robert Burns yearned ("To a Louse," 1786), it helps to see the person as someone else would see her. So I include a section entitled "Other People Say." I often customize it to identify the other person doing the seeing. For a business persona, I might use "Coworkers Say" or "Customers Say." In Aunt Millie's case, I've made it "Friends Say." And what her friends say is: "A little spacy. Talks best early in the day. Really proud of her grandchildren." This tells us she's older, she's family oriented, she's starting to lose it, and her friends are starting to adjust.

My other favorite personality cue is a user's pet peeve. As Frank Herbert asked in *Dune*, "What do you despise? By this are you truly known." If you want to understand someone, understand what he hates. And then put it into the persona, because it really helps you figure out what he's about. In Aunt Millie's case, it's "When the computer does all that stuff that it shouldn't do." Do you think that's vague, that it won't help you understand and help her? Her very inarticulate-ness speaks volumes for the kind of person that she is, and the way your program will have to work if you want to satisfy her.

Personal Essay

Finally, I've had a lot of success by including a personal essay written (purportedly) by the user herself. This allows the person to communicate with you directly. The essay doesn't have to be long. Five hundred words is plenty. Four hundred would be better.

It is extremely difficult to write in this form factor. You need to throw all your ideas onto the page, and then tighten, tighten, tighten. You need to be willing to delete sentences and even entire ideas. That can be difficult, because you fear that you might change your mind and want the deleted items later. This reluctance to delete anything will constipate your thoughts.

Here's a technique I've found for overcoming this block. For each essay you write, keep a separate file that contains the items you remove from the essay. You'll find it much easier to cut a sentence from the essay if you can paste it into this holder file instead of shredding it completely. I find that I rarely need to bring something back from the removed items file. But the ability to do so eases the initial removal, which is the key point.

Following is Aunt Millie's personal essay. Note the rambling, the difficulty in concentration, and the lack of what we would call "computer literacy skills." That's who *this* user is, and if you want her business, that's who you'll have to please.

I'm getting older. You never think it'll happen to you, but it does. I didn't think about it much when we buried my father some years ago. But putting my mother into a nursing home last year really made me stop and take stock of my life.

My mother is 92, and she's losing her marbles. Sometimes she recognizes me when I visit her; sometimes she thinks I'm her late sister, my Aunt Becky. That's how Alzheimer's goes, I guess.

She can remember stuff from her childhood really well, though, and we talk about that. Her siblings, and her parents, my grandparents, who I never really knew. And I'm thinking: Hey, I ought to be writing this down somewhere. She won't be around to say it much longer, and no one else remembers it now. And I don't know how much longer I'll be around, or able to remember it either.

My daughter's kids are five years old now, and they're asking, "Grandma, what were things like when you were a girl?" I think I want to get this all down somewhere so that they can see it. Maybe I can get them to help me, and we'll make it a project.

I have that computer the kids gave me a couple years ago. OK, I guess it was more like seven or eight. It has that Windows thing on it. I use it for email a little bit, or checking when stores are open, little stuff like that. My grandkids send me electronic greeting cards, which are nice. I'd still rather have a paper one that they made themselves, but that's today's kids for you. I don't trust any kind of online payment thing. I hear too much about bad guys stealing data and identities. My checkbook and stamps work just fine, and I don't lose sleep over them.

I tried writing everything down in Notepad, but that was hard and it didn't look good. I lost all the stuff I had typed in, several times, before I figured out this "saving" thing. And there's so much in my mother's boxes, like pictures and graduation programs and stuff, that Notepad can't deal with.

My geek nephew said he could find a program that would let me put it all on the computer. He installed it and tried to show me how to use it. He was pointing and clicking and dragging and dropping and all kinds of stuff I don't know how to do. The little kids tried to help, but I'm too slow for them. We all got really frustrated.

It's hard for me to see the screen, and my fingers don't move as well as they used to. I need something that doesn't jump around, something that stays there patiently until I'm ready to do something. Then I'd really like if it gave me some directions instead of waiting for me to figure stuff out. Because I often don't know where even to start.

This could be fun. But the computer programs need to get a lot better.

Using Personas

Now that we've constructed our persona, we need to display it in ways that our design and development staff will absorb and internalize. The size of this effort will obviously vary with the size and budget of the project, but here are a few ideas.

Don't just print it out and put it in a three-ring binder. I've seen this done, even done it myself. In today's electronic world, no one will ever look at it, let alone use it.

You want your persona to sink into your staff's subconscious minds. That means repetition. A good idea is to make some posters of the same persona, but with different pictures and taglines from the main persona. Most photographers produce multiple photos from a session with a model, so extras should be available without much trouble or expense. Figure 1.5 shows examples of this idea.

Winston

"Now this is not the end. It is not even the beginning of the end. But it is, perhaps, the end of the beginning."

Winston

"You ask, what is our aim? I can answer in one word: victory; victory at all costs, victory in spite of all terror, victory however long and hard the road may be; for without victory, there is no survival."

Figure 1.5 Additional posters of a persona.

As you'll see throughout this book, the UX design process is an iterative one. You don't just write a persona (or any other UX item, as we'll see in later chapters) and never touch it again. You update it as you gain new insights, adding new items and removing or correcting old ones. If you can change the posters, or at least move them around once in a while, that helps too.

To help this process, it is great if you can dedicate a specific wall space to the persona. You will put all the posters there (in addition to scattering them around), and the full persona write-up, with all the grokkability information and the personal essay. You want it in a location that gets lots of traffic.

You also want some way for passersby to contribute any ideas that the persona evokes, or submit new items that you ought to consider. A stack of sticky notes taped to the wall works well, along with a felt pen for scribbling (tied down so it won't disappear). Posted thoughts like "Stella's [military wife persona] husband just got new orders, time to move again" help a persona become real.

Succeeding with Personas

Let me tell you about a smashing victory I had in using personas. I was consulting for a company that was doing some cloud-related stuff. I constructed the persona of Robert "Don't Call Me Bob" Sherwood, to represent an older, conservative CIO, so my clients could understand the population they'd have to convince to go cloud. He's the guy scratching his head in Figure 1.2. He's the CIO of a supermarket chain, 62 years old, with three years left to retirement. Here's his personal essay:

> I'm Robert Sherwood. That's "Mr. Sherwood" to you. I'm CIO here at Super-Duper Market Stores. We're a family-owned local chain of 65 supermarkets, mostly inland in Southern California. You may never have heard of us, but we ranked #44 in Supermarket News's top retailers in 2013, with annual sales of approximately $3 billion.
>
> My boss came back recently from a trip and threw a *Business Week* magazine on my desk. The article said that companies could save 25% of their annual IT costs by moving to this cloud thing. MbM, "management by magazine," that's what I call it.
>
> We are never at the cutting edge of technological innovation. That's not our job. We let other companies step on the land mines. Our desktops are still on Windows XP. Call me a dinosaur. It does what I need it to do. It's already paid for. If I need something it doesn't do, I'll start looking then.
>
> The grocery industry is one of brutally low margins, often 4% or less. Lately it's been less more often than more. We need to conserve our capital for acquiring store sites and building new stores. That raises our gross sales and increases our purchasing volume,

thereby lowering our supplier prices and improving our margin just a little. We sure don't want to waste that on new computers.

The CEO has a bright nephew just out of business school, and a daughter who fancies herself a Web designer. They want to start a service where customers order their groceries online and we deliver them. Like FreshDirect in New York City, or Peapod in Massachusetts, they say. He's probably going to let them do it, and he'll want me to oversee it. Just what I need with three years until retirement. Not.

While I'm really not up to speed on the technologies they're proposing to use, I can provide the grocery business experience that they lack. They'll need to start small to make mistakes, then ramp up quickly if it takes off. Our current data center doesn't have the machines, the electricity, or even the floor space. We'll have to rent them somewhere. The kids keep talking "cloud." But if our customers' data gets hacked and it makes the evening news, not only is our delivery service toast, but our walk-in stores would take a huge hit too. To me, it's not worth the risk, but I've got my orders and my pension isn't fully vested yet, so I'm stuck. I sure hope this cloud thing doesn't blow up in my face.

When I read this essay to that company's technical staff, they grokked it immediately. Their chief architect said, "I see that Robert is taking a serious personal risk by using [our thing]. We have to make him feel comfortable with it." I knew that my persona had done its job.

CHAPTER 2

WHAT DO USERS WANT? (AND WHERE, AND WHEN, AND WHY?)

Now that we know who our users are, we turn our attention to what they want to do. What problems are they trying to solve, or what pleasurable state are they trying to enter?

In this chapter we see how to interview users to find out the answers to these and other questions. We also learn how to express them to the development team in the form of stories.

We're Not Programming Yet

In the first chapter, we figured out who our users really are—not ourselves, or who we wish they were or hope (futilely) that they'll somehow morph into. We then expressed that information in a format that our development team could digest and use: a persona.

We will do something similar in this chapter. We will figure out what our users really want or need from their software. What problem are they trying to solve, or what pleasurable state do they want to enter and maintain? And what would they consider to be the characteristics of a good solution or a good pleasurable state? We will then express this information in a format that our development team can digest and use: a story.

Did you think that being a UX geek was about programming? Wrong, my friend. For the first part of this process, we will be thinking like doctors. And for the second part, we'll be thinking like fiction writers.

After this, and only after this, can we start to say, "OK, now that we know who our users are and what they want, how close can we get to that with the technology that we have?" We will discuss this progression in later chapters.

But Users Don't Know What They Want!

I hear the same complaint in every UX class that I teach: "The users don't know what they want. How can we build it for them if they won't tell us?"

This isn't a new problem. In my first-ever industrial job, my boss circulated a poem entitled "The Night before Implementation." It ended with these lines:

> And the user exclaimed with a snarl and a taunt,
> "That's just what I asked for, but not what I want!"

That was 30 years ago, half the lifetime of the computing industry, and it probably wasn't new then.

Users have valuable information for us. Their satisfaction, and concomitant willingness to hand over their money, is our ultimate quality metric. But they don't know how to access and express that information in terms of UX, in the same way that medical patients don't know how to diagnose their own diseases. They can tell you if something feels good or bad once you ask them. But pulling the correct diagnosis out of the void isn't their problem. It's ours, trained professionals that we claim to be.

Think about it. When a patient goes to the doctor, he doesn't usually say, "I think I have type C fulminating leprosy, Kaminski variation." No. He says something like "Ow, my elbow hurts." It

Figure 2.1 The doctor is asking questions of his patient. (Photo © iStock.com/ monkeybusinessimages)

is the doctor's job to figure out what is causing the patient's elbow to hurt: did he bang it on something, or is cancer eating away at his bones, or is his wife cheating on him and he's displacing anxiety? Then, and only then, can the doctor decide whether to prescribe ibuprofen and ice packs, surgery and chemotherapy, or a divorce.

The patient doesn't know which pieces of information are important, or how to relate one piece to another. It is the doctor's job to ask the right questions (Figure 2.1): "Describe the pain for me. When did your elbow start hurting? What were you doing then? Does your other elbow hurt too? Does it hurt when I bend it this way? That way?" Lab tests and imaging may confirm the doctor's hypotheses, but all diagnosis stems from interviewing and examining the patient. This is a difficult skill to learn, and doctors who can do it well are good doctors.

So it is with us and our users. They don't come to us saying, "Jeez, I wish some animated character with bushy eyebrows would pop up at random intervals and say, 'It looks like you're about to crash. Don't you think you ought to save your work?'" Like the medical patient, our users express their feelings as best they can, usually beginning in a very general way, such as "I want to kill those bastards!" It is our job to ask the right questions to make the diagnosis, to figure out what's really hurting them so that we can make it stop. "Which bastards did you have in mind? What did they do specifically today to make you want to kill them?" and so on. Eventually, through our careful and patient probing, we can get the users to move past their immediate rage to identify its root causes: "I worked for three hours; then up came this stupid box saying, 'Microsoft Word has encountered an error and needs to close,' and all my work was gone."

This is a difficult skill to learn. User experience designers who can do it well are good designers. If there is one topic in this book in which success depends on experience, it would be this one. This chapter will start you in the right direction. But more than anything else in this book, it takes practice, practice, practice.

Finding Users to Examine

In order to figure out what users want and need, we have to talk to them. Talking to actual users is best if you can possibly reach them. But getting access to them can be trickier than you think.

USERS WANT US TO TALK TO THEM

You do not often associate government agencies with technological innovation, or with listening to and responding to their customers. But a student of mine, who works for a European government, returned from my class determined to change at least his little portion of the computing world: as I had taught him, he insisted on talking to the actual users. It wasn't easy to get to them. Their bosses said they were too busy. But he persisted and eventually set up some meetings.

He found that the user population was amazingly glad to be consulted. They didn't realize that good software was possible. They thought that software inherently had to suck; that's just how the world worked. They fully expected that the new system would be shoved down their throats like all the others, and they'd have to swallow it as they always did, warts and all. They never imagined that anyone would ask them how they worked or what they needed, what they did most often, where they got stuck, how they got moving again, and so on. My student reported to me that "the users are excited to be asked. Because they're not used to that at all. Shame on us." Amen.

It sometimes happens that you can't talk to your actual users. You wish you could, you know the outcome would be better, but damn it, you just can't get the access. For example, in the consulting business, it's (depressingly) common that the customer's IT team that is running the project will block direct access to users. They want to control the transaction, filtering everything through themselves, building what *they* want, rather than what the users want. Sometimes the users' boss is the obstacle.

I call this the "third-party problem": the party that's writing the check isn't the party using the software. Sometimes I call it the "Golden Rule problem": the guy with the gold makes the rules, and those rules get in your way. It's a tough problem, and you may never completely solve it, but here are workarounds with which you might find some success.

You need to come up with some sort of user representative or surrogate. Sometimes you can get the user population to delegate one. The thing you need to watch out for here is that often a person volunteers as a representative because she's a technophile—she's interested in software, she likes participating in the process; that's why she volunteered. The results that you get from her will then be skewed toward the technophilic, not necessarily the mainstream of your user group. Perhaps you can rotate the role of representative—this week it's one person, next week it's another. The changes can be disorienting at first, but you'll soon get an idea of the commonalities and variations within your user population.

Sometimes the users are just too tired to talk to you. This happens with industrial applications. These guys get off work and all they want to do is get out of the building and grab a cold brew. They don't want to spend time talking to some pointy-headed geek. You see this in the medical sector as well, where hours of unpaid overtime are depressingly common. In this case, finding their watering holes and buying a round of beer can get you started. After they've had a drink or two, asking, "What really burns you about XYZ software package?" will open the floodgates. *In vino veritas*, as they say.

If worse comes to worst, you can try hiring an outside subject matter expert. I was working on a medical application once and for a variety of reasons couldn't get to the actual users. I knew a nurse, who was employed at a different medical outfit and did the same sort of thing that the target users did. I offered to pay her to pick her brain about it. She found a few hours of moonlighting at consulting rates to be a much appreciated windfall. She's good at what she does, so perhaps our solution will contain an improved workflow.

Interviewing Users

Interviewing users or their representatives (Figure 2.2) is a critical skill. Doctors spend hours being taught to interview patients, and this process has been extensively studied. See, for example, "What Is a Successful Doctor-Patient Interview? A Study of Interactions and Outcomes" on PubMed.gov (www.ncbi.nlm.nih.gov/pubmed/6474233), which says (my emphasis added), "The physician's behaviour, *particularly that sort of behaviour which initiated a discussion such as an explicit request for the patient's opinion*, had more impact upon outcome than did the patient behaviour."

Figure 2.2 The UX medic is asking questions of his user. (Photo © iStock.com/Izabela Habur)

Above all, you have to get them started talking. Start by making your questions open-ended. Doctors are trained to open the conversation thus: "What brings you here today?" Following are some of the ways I get things moving:

- Tell me about yourself and your role here at Company A.
- What's the biggest problem you're trying to solve?
- What do you foresee as the biggest risks?
- What worries keep you awake at night?
- Tell me what really bothers you about (whatever).

As you continue the interview process, you will need to drill deeper. You still want to keep the questions as open-ended as possible, so as to get the maximum information from the user. Suppose you are developing a Web site for job searches. You might say, "Tell me about your new job." That will allow the user to tell you the types of things that matter to him. He might say something like "My kids are in the public schools, so I'm not willing to relocate. I'm looking to see what's within 20 or 30 miles of my house. Either that, or if they have really good telecommuting." You've gotten two pieces of information here: the sorts of things that cause a user to stay put, and one plausible alternative. If you had asked, "Do you want to search by title or salary range?" you wouldn't have learned either of these. Now that the user has opened this line of discussion, you probably want to follow up with something like "Interesting. Tell me more . . ." before moving on to another topic.

Be careful not to signal the answers that you want. You may well get the answer that you signal, but that answer may not be true. Here's one I got wrong back around 2004:

> **Me:** Haven't you always wanted your cell phone to give you driving directions?
>
> **My mother:** Nope. I can usually figure out where I am without much trouble, and if not, I ask someone. They often give me a nice cup of tea, too. I know you want me to say yes because you think it's so cool, but I don't really care. Sorry.

Someone less truthful than my mother, or perhaps more sparing of my feelings, would have reflected my enthusiasm and said, "Sure, that sounds kind of cool," even though she really didn't think so. And I'd have gone charging off after the wrong thing, at least for that demographic. (Obviously, a decade later, this technology has become ubiquitous on our smartphones.)

You will eventually narrow it down to more specific questions. As you do so, try to avoid misunderstandings caused by ambiguity. Don't ask, "Do you buy many music CDs nowadays?" Neither of you is sure how many CDs constitute "many." Instead, you might ask, "How many physical music CDs did you buy in the last six months? How many MP3 tracks?"

Observing Users

As Yogi Berra famously opined, "You can observe a lot by watching."[1] It's true. So if you're looking to learn what your users actually do, try watching them in their native habitat.

Watching users comes in two flavors: hidden and open. We're all familiar with the former. Many workers labor under the gaze of surveillance cameras more or less all day: bank tellers, cashiers, pharmacists, and many others (Figure 2.3). And many of our public spaces are under constant observation as well: shopping malls, transit centers, and so on. You can get a lot of objective information from watching these tapes—how many men and how many women got on a particular train, for example. You could do a time-and-motion study on the pharmacist—how often she went to this shelf, or to that one. It's one way to look at things and has some value. But for what we want to know, this isn't the best. The best comes from observing the users as they're doing their work, and talking with them about it.

This is open observation. In this case, you sit with the user and watch while she uses her current software. You can talk to her, and ideally get her to explain what she's doing and why (Figure 2.4).

Figure 2.3 Hidden observation. This pharmacy worker is constantly watched by cameras in the ceiling.

---

1. This quote appears in the title of Mr. Berra's book about teamwork (Wiley, 2009). It isn't one of the faux Yogi-isms, to which his autobiography, *The Yogi Book: I Really Didn't Say Everything I Said*, refers (Workman, 1999).

Figure 2.4   Open observation. This UX designer is working alongside a user to observe her operation. (Photo © iStock.com/hidesy)

This is what my European student did with his users. He sat next to them as they used the old system, asking, "What are you doing now?" They were happy to answer his questions, once they understood that he wasn't there to criticize them and their lack of computer literacy. He found that they didn't use the system all that often, so they didn't remember any sort of shortcuts. The interface had to be obvious to them every time, and the existing one wasn't. "We don't like this," they said. "It doesn't work like any other app we use. We don't use it all that often, so we have to figure it out again every time." My student was able to ask, "Do you think you'd rather scroll up and down on a single page, instead of jumping back and forth to different pages as it currently does?" to which the answer was a resounding "Yes!"

In some ways, this open observation resembles the usability testing we'll discuss in Chapter 4. You're sitting next to the user and watching while she uses the software. It's different in that here you're not assigning a task, as you do in usability testing. You are looking at what the user currently does. Also, the conversations with the user here are more two-way. In the usability test case, you ideally want a test run unpolluted by any outside output. In the current case, you are looking to see how the user manages to live in the polluted water.

> ### LAST WORD ON UX REQUIREMENTS GATHERING
>
> My father tells the following story about one of the first patients he ever treated. The ink wasn't dry on his MD diploma as he started his first job at the hospital clinic.
>
> A patient came in complaining, "I haven't had a bowel movement in a week." OK, thinks my dad. Bowel movement. No problem. Four years of medical school; I can handle this. He prescribed a mild laxative, but nothing happened. Tried a stronger one, still nothing. Getting a little frustrated, he tried an enema. Nothing came out. An ultrasound was negative, the blood work was unremarkable, an MRI scan didn't show anything. Getting desperate now, he took the patient up to the operating room and did an exploratory laparotomy—sliced open his abdomen to look around. Nothing to see; the patient had a completely normal belly. Finally, he did what he should have done in the first place: a thorough interview, during which he asked the patient what he did for a living. The patient said, "I'm a musician." Finally, the light bulb flashed on. "Ah! Of course!" exclaimed my dad. "Here's ten bucks. Go buy yourself something to eat."

Explaining It to the Geeks

Now that we have figured out what the user needs, we have to write it down in a way that we can use in the next stage of the process. That next stage will include mocking up screen layouts (Chapter 3) and refining them through user testing (Chapter 4). We'll generally iterate through that process several times. We will therefore find ourselves referring back to these requirements over and over again. We need to write them down in a form that we can digest and use.

There are two primary ways in which we could express user requirements. We could use a prescriptive approach, specifying every detail of what the geeks are to code. Specifications exist for this, such as IEEE-830:

- 4.6) The system shall allow a company to pay for a job posting with a credit card.
    - 4.6.1) The system shall accept Visa, MasterCard, and American Express cards.
    - 4.6.2) The system shall charge the credit card before the job posting is placed on the site.
    - 4.6.3) The system shall give the user a unique confirmation number.

This approach has several problems. First, simply creating and manipulating the formal structure consumes a great deal of time, like a flowchart. Also, it's hard to add new pieces as they arise, and they always arise. Invariably, as we will see, the user sees the first few pieces and says, "That's just what I asked for, but not what I want." It's hard to move things around once you've put them in.

The biggest problem, though, is that it's written from the system's point of view, rather than the user's point of view: "The system shall do [this]." We're not writing software for systems to use. We're writing for users. As you'll remember from the introduction, Avon had to junk a $125 million system because its UX was so awful that prospective users quit the company rather than touch it. A weasel spokesman said that Avon's order management system "is working as designed, despite any issues with the implementation of this project." That's what happens when you work from the system instead of the user.

This prescriptive approach is similar to the requirements of sacrificial practice laid out in the first book of Leviticus:

> [3] If the offering is a burnt offering from the herd, you are to offer a male without defect. You must present it at the entrance to the tent of meeting so that it will be acceptable to the Lord. [4] You are to lay your hand on the head of the burnt offering, and it will be accepted on your behalf to make atonement for you. [5] You are to slaughter the young bull before the Lord, and then Aaron's sons the priests shall bring the blood and splash it against the sides of the altar at the entrance to the tent of meeting. [6] You are to skin the burnt offering and cut it into pieces. [7] The sons of Aaron the priest are to put fire on the altar and arrange wood on the fire. [8] Then Aaron's sons the priests shall arrange the pieces, including the head and the fat, on the wood that is burning on the altar. [9] You are to wash the internal organs and the legs with water, and the priest is to burn all of it on the altar. It is a burnt offering, a food offering, an aroma pleasing to the Lord.

What can we do instead? We could start working from the user rather than the system. You describe the situation from the users' point of view, describing the participants, their actions, and the results. Continuing the biblical analogy, think of the parable of the Good Samaritan, here from the Gospel of Luke, Chapter 10:

> [29] [An expert in law] asked Jesus, "And who is my neighbor?"
>
> [30] In reply Jesus said: "A man was going down from Jerusalem to Jericho, when he was attacked by robbers. They stripped him of his clothes, beat him and went away, leaving him half dead. [31] A priest happened to be going down the same road, and when he saw the man, he passed by on the other side. [32] So too, a Levite, when he came to the place and saw him, passed by on the other side. [33] But a Samaritan, as he traveled, came where the man was; and when he saw him, he took pity on him. [34] He went to him and bandaged his wounds, pouring on oil and wine. Then he put the man on his own donkey, brought him to an inn and took care of him. [35] The next day he took out two denarii and gave them to the innkeeper. 'Look after him,' he said, 'and when I return, I will reimburse you for any extra expense you may have.'

36 "Which of these three do you think was a neighbor to the man who fell into the hands of robbers?"

37 The expert in the law replied, "The one who had mercy on him." Jesus told him, "Go and do likewise."

When asked the technical question of who exactly is a neighbor, Jesus didn't reply with a specification. One who lives next door? A blood relationship out to second cousin once removed? No. He told a story. He used a specific example, hypothetical actions of fictional characters, to illustrate a general principle. He invited the listener to place himself in the shoes of the characters to think about what the underlying principle meant. It's an extension of the persona principle, whereby we concocted an artificial person to illustrate our user population. We will now give these personas actions and results to describe the needs of our user population. We will tell stories.

Storytelling

Storytelling is the oldest communication mechanism known to humankind. It exists in every culture, ancient and modern. As Joan Didion wrote in her novel *The White Album*, "We tell ourselves stories in order to live. The princess is caged in the consulate. The man with the candy will lead the children into the sea. . . . We live entirely by the imposition of a narrative line upon disparate images."

The term *story* gets thrown around a lot in the UX business. It's a very generic word. As always, when a generic word gets used to label a specific situation, no one agrees on exactly what the thing is or isn't. (*Object* is the classic example.)

So it is with the term *story*. One development shop calls a certain thing a story, but to a different shop, "No, that's not a story. That's a use case [or maybe a scenario]. A story is something else." This book uses the word *story* in its most generic sense: "a narrative, either true or fictitious, in prose or verse, designed to interest, amuse, or instruct the hearer or reader." (I won't be writing mine in verse, though it might be kind of cool if I could. Try it sometime and tell me what you get.)

Expressing our requirements through stories allows other users to read and understand them. Stories stick in human minds better. We can discuss and refine them iteratively as we proceed through the design process. And they keep implementation detail, undesirable at this stage, from obscuring the broadest issues.

Writing Stories

You've seen stories everywhere throughout your life. Wasn't that one of your very first sentences: "Grandpa, tell me a story"? No doubt you've told plenty of them. But you probably haven't thought about them as input to the design process. What does this sort of story need?

Think about newspaper reporters. What information are they taught to find, and then compose into their stories? The fundamental questions: Who? What? Where? When? And then, if they're thinking a little more deeply, Why? We'll be doing that in our user story work. Then, and only then, can we proceed to How?

We dedicated all of Chapter 1 to working out Who? So you can generally start your story with a persona name—"Bob," "Aunt Millie," whoever it is.

The next most important question is What? What problem is Aunt Millie trying to solve, or what pleasurable state does she want to enter? What does she consider to be the characteristics of a good solution or pleasurable state? You'll generally start with some sort of scene setting to describe the problem and some sort of goal setting to specify the sort of action she wants, and the goal she wants to achieve. As I said before, the key is to write these from the user point of view, not the system point of view. For example:

> "Aunt Millie's sciatica is really kicking up, worse than before. She wants to find some exercises that might help stretch her hip out and make it stop hurting, or at least hurt less."

We can add information further describing the problem and its solution:

> "The pain isn't too bad when she's resting on the couch, but it hurts when she walks even as far as the bathroom."

We can add grokkability information, as we did in the persona:

> "She's out of oxycodone and can't get any more until her doctor's appointment two days hence."

If we know anything at this stage about the desired solution, we can put it in as well:

> "Aunt Millie saw a yoga instructor once demonstrate exercises that she said helped with hip pain. She didn't think much of it at the time, but now she's willing to try anything."

You have a pretty good idea of what Aunt Millie is going through, and what she wants done, don't you? You sympathize with her. You want to help her. It's short, but it's a good first cut at a story.

Remember, our stories are not saying anything about implementation. We will definitely *not* say things like "The database tables shall be named Customers and Products." Nothing about iFrames and Divs. And goodness knows, nothing about HTTP versus HTTPS.

Interview and Story Example

Suppose you were working on the UX for your public library's Web site, to improve the experience of borrowing the electronic books that make up an increasing part of its circulation today. Suppose that, through a user survey, you found that 80% of the patrons who use electronic books do so in Amazon's Kindle format. Either they have actual Kindle devices or they use a Kindle reader app on other devices.

Now you start talking to a live user. Perhaps you got in contact with that user by waiting patiently in a library room, having asked the librarians to direct any interested patrons your way.

> **You:** Tell me about reading library books on your Kindle. [What, most general]
>
> **Bob:** Well, I really like it. It means that I can get books without having to go to the library.
>
> **You:** Sounds interesting. What do you like best about library books on your Kindle? [What, refined somewhat]
>
> **Bob:** I travel a lot. I especially love my Kindle when I go away on business trips or vacations. I can load it up with library books when I leave and read them at the airport or on the plane or in the hotel. I used to have to carry all my books in my pack, but now they all fit on this Kindle. I can even reload it from the road if I'm out long enough to finish them all, but I'm usually not.
>
> **You:** Cool. Tell me more. [Inviting further discussion, What and Why]
>
> **Bob:** I'm a cheapskate, and books are expensive now, so I borrow more from the library and buy fewer of them. The library mostly lends hardcovers, which take up more space and weight in my pack. And I'm afraid I'll forget one in a hotel room, which would wipe out any sort of cost savings. As long as I have my Kindle, I've got everything with me. Man, that Jeff Bezos guy has it. I wonder if that *New York Times* article bothers him, about the brutal culture at Amazon. Maybe his *Washington Post* will attack it!
>
> **You (getting back on track):** When would you say you most often download books to your Kindle? [When, also Where]
>
> **Bob:** I usually head out on a Sunday. It's a pain in the ass to get everything packed up. And I can never get to the bookstore or the library in time. And their hardcover books are heavy

anyway. [This repetition is good. Don't roll your eyes. Nod sympathetically.] I'm always running around trying to get ready.

You (guessing): So you're at home packing up, and you want to load up your Kindle too? [When and Where, reconfirmation]

Bob: Yes, the library Web site is much easier to use on a PC than on a mobile device. They're a nonprofit—I guess they can't afford a good usability study—so it really sucks on a phone or tablet. And you can't depend on Internet connections when you travel. I like to be loaded up before I go. If I can't, then I can't, but I'd rather.

You: What kinds of books do you like best? [What, Why, keep the guy talking]

Bob: [Whatever, it doesn't matter]

You: Do they have a lot of those in the electronic library?

Bob: Actually they don't have that many. Their electronic collection is new in the last couple of years, and they are just starting to expand it. There'll be more in the future. The library director says they're spending half their new book budget on electronic books. They're actually quite expensive if you're acquiring library loan rights.

You: Is it hard to find the ones you want? [What, When, possibly a new story]

Bob: You can put a hold on anything they have in their collection, and it will automatically show up on your Kindle when it's available. Sometimes it takes a while for your request to get to the front of the queue. I hate having to browse and browse and browse and see all these books not available. That's especially annoying when I'm loading up to head out.

You: So you'd like some way to restrict your selections to what's currently available? [What, Why]

Bob: Yes, that'd be great. Oh, and one more thing. The librarian at the brick building has a shelf of books to read instead of popular ones that take a long time to get. Waiting for the new Jack Reacher from Lee Child? Try David Poyer, or maybe Stephen Hunter. Stuff like that. It'd be great when I'm loading up to head out and don't have a whole lot of time to fart around choosing. Just toss something onto my stack and head on out.

You: So you're asking for automatic recommendations among what's available to you right now? [What, Why]

Bob: Yes, that's it.

After thinking through Bob's responses carefully, you might write the following story:

Bob travels a lot for his job. It's Sunday afternoon, and Bob is packing up for another business trip. He reads a lot on these trips, in the airport and on the plane and at the hotel, or while eating alone in restaurants. When he travels, he likes to bring books on his Kindle, because it's small and light and convenient. He wants to get his Kindle books from his public library because it's cheap. As part of his packing, he logs in to the library

Web site to see what they have for him. Many of the electronic titles are checked out right now, so he selects "Show Only Available Titles." The display resets to show these. One or two of them catch his eye, and he selects them. He then is interested in some new things, so he clicks "Show Recommendations." A list appears, based on [whatever criteria we decide]. He moves through the choices and selects the maximum the library will allow him to check out at a time. He tosses his Kindle into his pack and heads out to make a living.

Writing the initial story is generally not the last word. As you go through mockup development (Chapter 3) and usability testing (Chapter 4), you will learn new things about your users and the problem they're really trying to solve. The testing will refine the mockups. And it's not unusual that the refined mockups will refine these stories as well. Don't consider that a failure. And to this iteration we now turn our attention.

CHAPTER 3

SKETCHING AND PROTOTYPING

Having worked our way through the first three chapters, we now have a decent idea of who our user is, what problem our user is trying to solve, and what our user would consider to be the characteristics of a good solution. It is now time to start creating and refining the potential solutions to this particular problem for this particular user.

It's an ongoing, iterative process. The only way to succeed is to fail: fail early, fail often, fail cheaply. Cheap, disposable sketches are the way to make that happen.

Prototyping: The Wrong Way to Start

The biggest mistake I see developers make is this: when it's time to start working on solutions, they immediately fire up a full application developer tool, such as Visual Studio or Expression Blend or Xamarin Studio. They use that tool to create a new skeleton application project, be it desktop or Web or mobile. They then immediately start dragging controls from the palette onto the design surface—a button here, a check box there; what do you think, should this be a dropdown list or a set of radio buttons? Then they start adding code to it to demonstrate some of its functionality—having a button bring up a dialog box, maybe connecting a grid to display data from a dummy database. Then they show it to their developer peers, not the users or their representatives, for feedback. The peers, busy with their own projects, always nod and say, "Yeah, looks pretty good."

When asked why they do this, developers are puzzled. "What kind of question is that?" they say. "We're building an application. This is the tool that we use. What else did you have in mind?"

What the devs are doing is constructing a prototype. A prototype is an actual product that more or less works—perhaps not perfectly, probably needing some refinements, but it works from one end to the other. A prototype airplane actually does fly. You test the prototype to confirm that it flies as far and as fast as your calculations say that it should. If it doesn't, you still have a chance to fix the problem before you produce thousands of them and deliver them to customers. Figure 3.1 shows a prototype US Air Force F-35 fighter testing its ability to restart its engine in flight. But this isn't the way to start designing a user experience.

Figure 3.1 This prototype F-35 is being tested for its ability to restart the engine in flight. (US Air Force photo, www.edwards.af.mil/shared/media/photodb/photos/081023-F-3571D-400.jpg)

Starting with a Good Sketch

The medium of software is almost infinitely tractable. In the words of Frederick Brooks, we are working with "nearly pure thought-stuff." We have a few physical constraints, such as the size of the display area and the types of input devices. But apart from that, we can put almost anything into our app. Figuring out what ought to be programmed is as hard as actually programming it.

It is extremely difficult to put ourselves into our users' shoes, to know what they'll like and understand and find useful and (we hope) buy. We can make guesses, educated by our user research and interviews, personified via personas and stories. But the only way we can know how good our guesses are is to actually show them to users and get feedback. We incorporate their suggestions, refine our design, and get feedback again. This iterative process is the only way to produce a design that works.

The type of feedback we get from users is astounding. They give us initial input, but they don't realize what they know until they actually see it in front of them. "Yes, I'm doing this thing here, but now I need this piece of data. Didn't I mention that? Oh, sorry. But I need it now. Where is it? On another screen, you say? That's no good. Bring it to me now. Where should it go? Maybe get rid of this thing here, which I'm not using." And so on.

Users themselves can't tell us the first time around what they need or want. They need to have their minds jogged, their ideas stirred around, by specific examples. You probably remember the old night-before-implementation spoof poem:

> And the user exclaimed with a snarl and a taunt,
> "That's just what I asked for, but not what I want."

The only way to solve this problem is to try many different ideas. And because we need to do that, we need to do so quickly and cheaply. We will therefore start by making sketches instead of prototypes. A sketch is a simple, quickly executed drawing that illustrates essential concepts without providing details. Think of what you see an artist do with just a few strokes of a pencil, as in Figure 3.2.

A sketch is intended to suggest ideas to the test users, to stimulate their imagination and thought process. "Do you like this? What about that? Why? Why not? Do you not like this because the font is too small or because you're not thinking about these things at this time?" and so on.

Above all, you want the sketch to appear temporary. You are not looking to produce anything reusable at this point. You want the test users to feel free to say, "Change this."

Figure 3.2   A good early sketch—just a few simple strokes evoke the entire butterfly. (Photo © iStock.com/red_frog)

When users see the sketch, they'll often contradict something that they told you in an interview. "I know I said I wanted this, but now that I see it here, it just doesn't fit. Get rid of it; we'll see it on another screen maybe." That's not something to get upset about. It's just the way humans are. Be happy that you found it out now, early in the process, so you can do something about it.

You especially do not want any code at this point, because if the UX changes, the code will have to change as well. That takes time, costs money, and makes you more reluctant to explore something interesting or abandon something that hasn't proved useful.

Imagine you had a set of radio buttons with rudimentary code behind them. Suppose a reviewer said, "I don't like those radio buttons. They take up too much space, and all those names distract me when I'm trying to think. And I don't change them often anyway." You reply, "How about turning them into a dropdown list?" and the test user agrees. Now you have to change the code that selected the initial radio button and responded to clicks on the set and replace it with code for managing a list. Changing that code has a larger cost than just changing a drawing. And because it has a larger cost, you are more reluctant to try that change, and users are more reluctant to suggest it.

In general, you want to keep these sketches in monochrome. If you start putting in colors, the users to whom you show the sketches will think immediately about the color and not about other things. "Hmm, I don't know about that blue. Could it maybe be a little more green?" You don't want them thinking about it at this stage of the game. That's for the graphic designers, otherwise known as the decorators, and it happens at the very end.

The process of creating and refining sketches until we get to one we like resembles a funnel (see Figure 3.3). We start with a number of ideas covering a wide range of possibilities. (a) "Are you thinking more in terms of menus or tabs? Or maybe a toolbar?" We'll show them to users and get feedback. "Now that I see them on the screen, I think tabs work the best for what we're

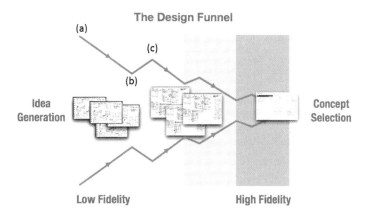

Figure 3.3   The design funnel. (Courtesy Balsamiq)

doing here." So we throw out all the sketches involving menus and toolbars (b).[1] Then we'll develop the remaining ideas about tabs, adding some detail, expanding the choices among the remaining elements (c): Two tabs or three? At the top or bottom of the screen? We'll repeat the process, getting feedback, winnowing down the choices, and so on. Eventually, we'll wind up with the concept that we're going to implement (three tabs at the bottom of the screen).

As we improve our concept, we increase the fidelity of the representation. At the beginning, we might use an empty rectangle to indicate a toolbar. As we move ahead, and the toolbar survives more of the winnowing process, we might sketch a few buttons on it. At the end, the toolbar would probably contain all its controls with their labels.

Mockup Tool Example: Balsamiq

Now you're starting to think about making these sketches, and of course you're freaking out. Sketch? That's what art majors do when they get a break from flipping hamburgers: sketch pigeons in the alley and hope that someday their talent will be discovered. "I'm a geek; I use computers for everything," you're thinking to yourself. "Do I have to start carrying around a paper sketch pad and a pencil, even—God help me—an eraser?"

Of course not. Very good software tools exist for sketching a UX layout. They're just not built into the major development tool packages, which are geared toward producing code. You want a sketching package that makes simple things very, very simple; very, very fast; and very, very cheap. You want the sketches thus produced to be disposable and to appear disposable, so

---

1. You probably want to move the menu and toolbar sketches out of your mockup project so they don't distract you from looking at the tabs. But you probably don't want to completely erase them, in case you want to circle back later. I often keep a file called "Removed Ideas" for each project that I'm working on, for this express purpose.

reviewers feel free to suggest changes. You don't want them to tempt you toward prematurely producing code.

These sketching tools produce a low-fidelity representation of a proposed screen layout. The terms used to describe this layout vary. So far we've used the generic term *sketch*, though as you see, it has paper-and-pencil connotations we should avoid. You will sometimes hear *wireframe* as a generic term for a low-fidelity representation. This too has specific connotations from the early days, meaning a three-dimensional model that showed a figure's outlines without the computationally intensive task of rendering its surfaces. To avoid these confusing connotations, this book will henceforth use the term *mockup* to mean a low-fidelity representation of a user experience layout produced by a software tool.

One useful mockup editor is Balsamiq Mockups (www.balsamiq.com). The desktop version costs $89 for a one-user license. Its closest competitors are MockFlow and Axure. Balsamiq produces mockups like Microsoft WordPad produces documents—with quick, cheap, basic functionality. Neither provides the capability of deep diving, as Expression Blend does for drawing (see databinding class diagrams) and Microsoft Word does for writing (see the equation editor). This simplicity is a feature, not a bug, for our needs at this stage of the UX process.

With Balsamiq, you will find it very easy to produce quick mockups of your UX ideas. You will also find it easy to copy a mockup and make small changes to it, so you can examine a great many different ideas very quickly. Rather than spend more time describing it, let's look at a quick example.

You might remember Nextel, a wireless phone carrier in the United States before Sprint bought it in 2005. Nextel provided standard cell phone service like the other carriers, but its primary attraction to customers was its unique "push-to-talk" feature. The user would press and hold a button on his handset while talking into the mouthpiece, similar to a walkie-talkie radio. The call would be automatically directed to the Nextel phone or group of phones that the user had preconfigured. The recipients would hear an alert tone, then the caller's voice, without having to touch their phones. The original caller would release his button when he was finished talking, at which time the recipient could press his button to talk back to the caller.

This communication pattern fit a certain operational niche very well. It had almost a cult following among customers who needed frequent, short interactions among a small set of users who moved around a lot—the dispatcher of a small fleet of vehicles, say, or a contractor, or a caterer.

Or a medical examiner. Shiya Ribowsky worked as a medicolegal investigator for the New York City Medical Examiner's Office. In his book *Dead Center* (Harper Collins, 2007), he wrote about their staff responding on 9/11, charging downtown before the towers fell, "all equipped with Nextel phones and two-way radios. . . . At the office, we listened over the phones and radios to our seasoned co-workers crying as they watched people jump from the burning towers."

You can't buy these phones anymore. But many users swore by them. Suppose we wanted to re-create them in today's smartphone environment, like the dinosaurs in *Jurassic Park*. The key, of course, is getting the UX right. So here are some mini-personas and a mini-story to jump-start this design:

The carpenters who built my house absolutely loved the Nextel walkie-talkie phone. I spent a lot of time watching them use it and discussing it with them. They were really angry when Sprint discontinued it.

Imagine the boss man, Todd, and his employees, Pete, Jimmy, and Bob. They're skilled carpenters, they're busy as heck, and in their own words, "We don't have time to fart around." Some days they'll all work on one site; some days they're spread out among several sites. Sometimes Todd has to stay back at the office to do paperwork, or visit prospective clients to bring in new business. These guys need to talk to each other dozens of times per day, for example:

> **Pete (presses to talk to all users):** Guys, I'm at the hardware store. How many boxes of those nails do you need? [releases talk button]
>
> **Bob (hears alert tone, hears Pete's request, presses talk button):** Get me three boxes, OK? [releases button]
>
> **Jimmy (hears Pete and Bob, presses talk):** I'll need a couple more next week, so how about you grab them now? [releases button]
>
> **Todd (hears entire conversation, presses talk):** That store gives a discount for ten boxes, so get that many. We'll use them soon. [releases button]

If Sprint won't sell phones with walkie-talkies anymore, why not just do a conference call via Skype, or the cell carrier's own connection? Partly it's simplicity. Pushing a dedicated button is faster than bringing up an app and selecting a contact, even one on speed dial. And hearing the caller's voice without needing to answer saves some time as well. When you do it 50 times a day, those savings add up. Partly it's the ability to speak to a group of contacts directly. A taxi dispatcher saying, "Hey, who's near 15th Street?" could just tap a button and speak, without waiting for the recipients to answer. Anyone with his phone turned on will hear the incoming message without having to answer it. He doesn't have to touch his phone if it's not something he needs to respond to. Skype makes many more operations possible than the simple walkie-talkie case. But these simplest of operations are no longer as simple as they were.

When I tell this story to developers, I invariably get howls of protest: "But Skype lets you do X! And Y! Why don't those dumb users want those things? Sounds like we need to educate them." Wrong, my geeky friend. Your user is not you. These users would rather have the ultra-simplicity in their most common case than fancy features in less common cases. If you want their money, you have to give them what they want.

"They said that if we liked our cell phones, we could keep our cell phones," complains Todd. "No, wait a minute, that was our health plan. But why do they insist on wrecking something that we were fine with?"

Like it or not, smartphones are what we have today. A few apps, such as Voxer, claim to provide the previous functionality on a modern platform, but users of those apps know that no, they're not the good old thing. As with most modern apps, they are loaded with features, and the old simplicity gets lost. Suppose we wanted to provide a bare-bones walkie-talkie app to make Todd and his crew happy? Let's sketch out what it might look like, show it to some users, and see what they think.

Understand that we are sketching out the UX solely from the user's point of view. We're not talking about designing the underlying communication functionality. We do not care what sort of gyrations the communication engineers go through to make it work the way our users want, what sort of five-dimensional hyper-pretzels they have to contort themselves into. If the engineers squawk (and they probably will when they see the simplicity of the UX instead of the feature bloat that such geeks prefer), we'll fall back on Plattski's Universal Geek Challenge Remedy: "What? You mean you're not smart enough?"

We could construct some layouts in Visual Studio or Expression Blend. But learning and then using these very powerful environments takes a whole lot longer than doing the same thing in Balsamiq. The finished appearance of controls would make the users less willing to suggest changes. And it would encourage us to start coding the UX prematurely. So we're going to mock up our layouts in Balsamiq instead.

We open the desktop version of Balsamiq, shown in Figure 3.4. There's a list of all our mockups on the left. Currently we have only one, labeled "New Mockup 1." The column on the right contains a place for notes about this mockup. Our work surface is in the middle. Across the top you see a toolbar with the outlines of the different symbol objects that Balsamiq knows about; we can drag and drop these onto the work surface.

This app is intended for a smartphone, so we probably want to start with some sort of phone-shaped frame. Looking on the symbol toolbar, we see one for an iPhone. We haven't yet thought about whether this app should aim for Android or iPhone, or if we should even consider Windows phones. But that doesn't matter at this stage of the mockup design. We're at the largest opening of the design funnel. So we press and hold the left mouse button on the iPhone symbol, drag it onto the work surface, and release the left mouse button to drop the symbol where we want it. The results are shown in Figure 3.5.

Note that Balsamiq deliberately shows the outline in a sketchy sort of rendering. For example, the home button at the bottom is not perfectly rectangular, nor is the circle around it completely circular. This lack of fidelity suggests to your subconscious mind that this is a cheap, disposable mockup. You couldn't ship a product with this makeshift appearance. It is, and appears to be, purely a mockup.

On the right side, you now see a window showing the editable properties of this iPhone layout. You can see such choices as the iPhone 4 or iPhone 5, and landscape or portrait orientation. The differences between the iPhone versions are small enough that we can ignore them for now.

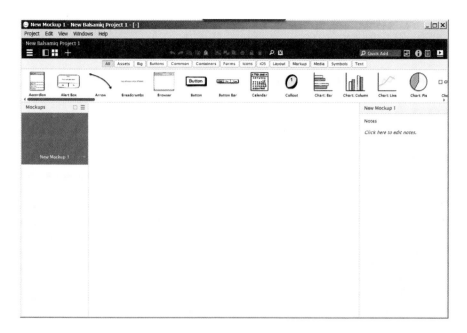

Figure 3.4   Empty Balsamiq project, initial mockup.

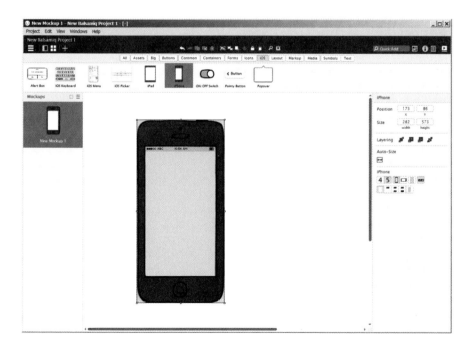

Figure 3.5   Balsamiq project with the iPhone outline.

Phones are almost always used in portrait orientation while talking, so we'll leave that setting intact as well. Again, remembering the design funnel we saw earlier in this chapter, we don't want to spend time on these details now.

The location and size of the phone are shown in PC screen pixels. The actual resolution of an iPhone 6 display is 1136 x 640 pixels, about double what Balsamiq is showing. The pixels on phones, particularly iPhones, are more densely packed than on most PC monitors. That lack of fidelity is precisely not the point here. We're not going to spend time matching pixel for pixel. We are looking to do a relatively large number of layouts, quickly and cheaply, so we can decide which ones we want to spend time developing further. We can zoom in (Ctrl +) for a closer look, or out (Ctrl -) for a wider one.

How should we start? What would the simplest design be? Well, this app is about frequently calling a small number of people, the same ones all the time. So let's plan from the very beginning to optimize this case. How about putting some large buttons on the app's home screen for quick access? Maybe with contact names in them?

Let's select the Button control from the UI library toolbar, drag it, and drop it on the screen. When we do this, the data entry editor for the button opens, so we can type in the text that we want it to display. In this case, it's "Bob," the employee we want the button to call. The right column now shows the properties of the new text area. The default is centered, which is what you expect from a button most of the time. The button's size is automatically set to the size of the text string (Figure 3.6).

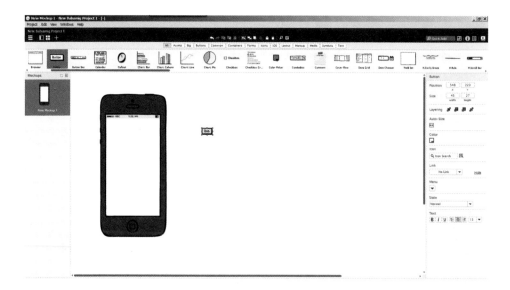

Figure 3.6   Balsamiq project with the iPhone outline and one button.

We now need to figure out the size and arrangement of buttons within the phone. Remember, we're talking about fast access to a small, tight group. We don't want to spend time scanning a long list. Carpenters work with their hands, so they tend to have larger fingers with less fine control. So how about something large, say, two columns, with maybe three or four buttons in each? Let's drag Bob's button into the iPhone layout and size it to take up about half the width. We'll adjust its height to where it looks and feels good to us. The text string will probably get small, so we'll use the properties window to adjust its font. Twenty-four point looks OK for now (Figure 3.7).

Now that we have one button in our iPhone layout, we want to add more buttons. To make them the same size as the first one, we'll just click on that button to select it, type Ctrl-C to copy, then Ctrl-V to paste. We repeat Ctrl-V two more times, giving us a total of four buttons. We drag the new ones to form a square arrangement in the mockup. Then we double-click each button to edit its text string. We can change "Bob" to "Pete," "Jimmy," and "Everyone." Oops, the legend "Everyone" doesn't quite fit this button size in 24-point font. What to do? Change its font size maybe? Or add a \n character into the text which splits it onto two lines? Change its name to "All"? We'll try one of those; if we don't like it, we'll try another. But above all, we won't spend much time fiddling with it. Now we have what's shown in Figure 3.8. The touch zones are large, and the button names are too. The buttons are easy to see and easy to tap, hard to screw up. Simple, as a walkie-talkie should be.

We now have one mockup to show to some potential users. Let's try another type of layout to see which they like better. Suppose we wanted to explore the possibility of using photos on our buttons instead of just the contact's name. That's a common feature on many cell phones

Figure 3.7 Balsamiq project with the iPhone outline and one button in the layout.

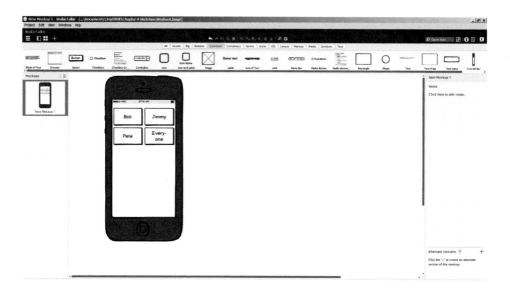

Figure 3.8   Balsamiq project with the iPhone outline and multiple recipient buttons.

today. On the other hand, the reason these customers are demanding this app is a return to the simple old days. Which would they prefer, pictures or just text? I don't know. And I won't believe you if you say that you know. In fact, I don't think I'd believe the users if they told me without seeing it first. Fortunately, we can mock this up quite easily and show it to them.

If we right-click on our mockup in the Mockups list on the left side, we'll see a context menu with the choices of Rename and Duplicate. We'll click Duplicate, and it will make a copy of the existing mockup (Figure 3.9). You tend to get a lot of these cloned mockups because it's so easy to do. We might as well give it a name right now, at creation time. So a descriptive name is a good idea. However, not too much of the name shows in the list, so very long ones get clipped. Try to make mockup names distinctive in the first couple of dozen characters. We'll call this new one "Picture Buttons." (While we're at it, we might as well change the name of the first mockup, perhaps to "Text-Only Buttons," as shown.)

Now we start putting in buttons that could contain pictures. How do we get these? Balsamiq doesn't supply an image button on the control list. We could try pasting a picture onto a regular button, but Balsamiq doesn't allow us to change the vertical position of the text. We could drag a rectangle symbol into each button location, and a label, and a picture, four times or more. But that would get complicated, and we'd have to keep repositioning and resizing all of the sub-items, especially as we develop the idea further.

Fortunately, we can simulate an image button by making a *group*. This is a logical combination of several Balsamiq control symbols that we manipulate as a unit. Again, it's easier to show you one than to describe it. We select a rectangle control and drag it onto the design surface. We

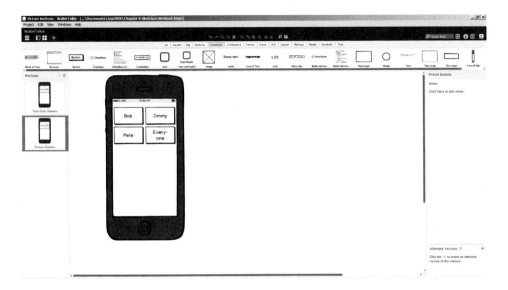

Figure 3.9 Balsamiq project with a cloned mockup to use for picture buttons.

adjust its size to be the same as that of the button controls we used previously. Now we're ready for the picture. We could use an image control, which can display a picture of any type. But it's easier to use the control called Webcam, which already contains a caricature of a person's face. We drag a webcam control into the rectangle and adjust its size. We still need a name, so we drag a label control into the box. We adjust its position underneath the webcam control and set its text to "Jimmy."

Now that we have these together, we want to tie them together so that we can manipulate them as a unit—drag and drop, position, size, and so on. That's quite easy. We select all three of these items—the rectangle, the label, and the webcam picture—in the standard Windows way, by holding down the Control key and clicking each item. When we have them all selected, we click the Group button on the toolbar, as shown in Figure 3.10.

Now, all three of these controls are bound together in a group. We can click just once to select the group, move it around, and position it wherever we want. The group sizes as a unit, more or less. We can copy the group as a unit and paste several groups into the new mockup, as we did before with the buttons—Ctrl-C, then Ctrl-V three times. We drag each group where we want it, more or less where the buttons are in the other mockup.

But wait. What about changing the text? We surely don't want four buttons to say "Jimmy," do we? Of course not (unless we *really* like Jimmy). We can edit the internal items of a group without ungrouping them. If we double-click on the group, we enter a mode in which we can change the contents of the group. If we then double-click on Label with the group, it opens up the text editor, so we can change the label's contents (Figure 3.11).

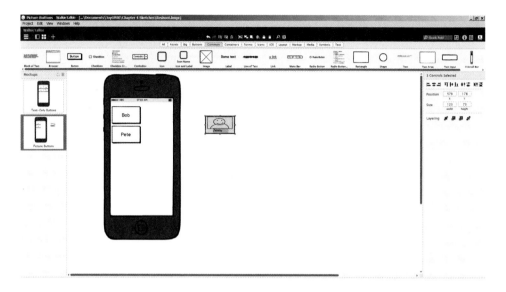

Figure 3.10 Balsamiq project with a custom button being grouped.

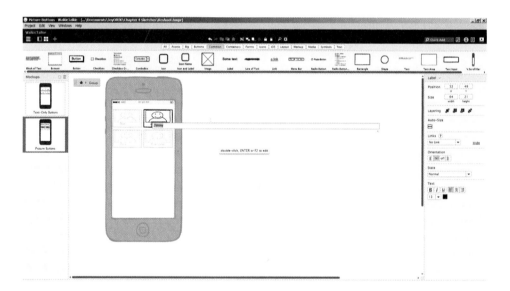

Figure 3.11 Balsamiq project, changing the label text inside a custom button group.

That's all we'll look at with layouts in Balsamiq. There is a whole tutorial on the Balsamiq Web site, exercising each part of the editor product. However, don't spend too much time on tutorials—just jump in, and consult the documentation only as you get stuck.

Showing Interaction through a Storyboard

Each static image shows the UX at a particular point in time. But to effectively communicate a user's ongoing actions, we often need to show several screens in a connected sequence. We do that by pasting mockups side by side on a single panel, known as a *storyboard*. Let's see how a storyboard can help us discover and fix an important problem in our walkie-talkie cell phone app example.

More than anything else, we learned that Nextel's former users liked its extreme simplicity. Todd would pull out his phone, press a single button, and say, "Pete?" Pete would hear Todd, pull out his own phone, press a single button, and say, "Yeah, Todd?" No swiping, no scrolling, no tap dancing, no nothing. Push the button and there's the guy.

So far, we've thought of our walkie-talkie app as a regular smartphone app. We'd launch it from the phone's home screen. We've never questioned this unconscious decision—it's for a smartphone, so it's an app like all the others. But when we make up a storyboard of the connection process and present it to nostalgic Nextel users, we'll discover that it leaves them underwhelmed. Look at the storyboard shown in Figure 3.12.

> **note**
>
> I produced this storyboard in Microsoft Word. I set the page orientation to landscape and inserted a table, with two rows and six columns. I copied each image from Balsamiq into the Clipboard ("Project→Export→Mockup to Clipboard"—Balsamiq's menus are often a little bit strange) and pasted them into the cells in the lower row of the table.

Todd's Phone

(a)Todd pulls out phone, sees blank screen	(b)Todd Presses 'On' button, sees phone lock screen	(c)Todd swipes on, sees phone home screen	(d)Todd selects Walkie-Talkie app, if it's not already running, sees our home screen	(e)Todd taps desired contact or group, in this case Pete. App connects.	(f)Todd talks into the phone: "Hey, Pete?"

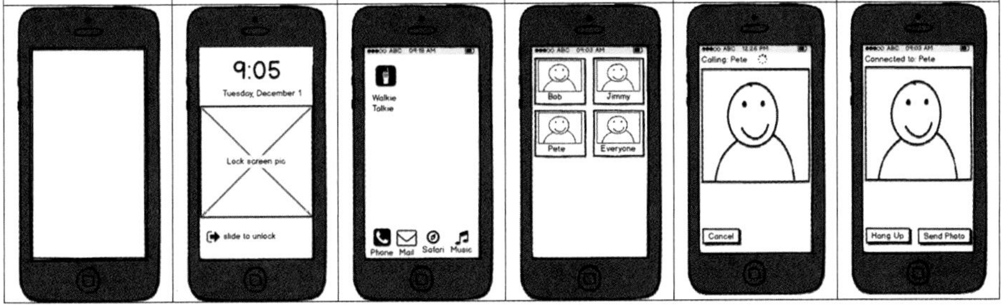

Figure 3.12 Storyboard showing the sequence of interaction.

As in a comic strip, each cell shows the mockup of the screen after one sequential user action. The caption on the top explains what the user has done to get to this position. We take the simplest case where Todd wants to talk to Pete. He pulls out his phone and sees the blank screen (a). He taps the On button. Now he sees the phone's lock screen (b). Todd swipes into the phone and sees the phone's home screen (c). Now he has to select our walkie-talkie app, if it's not already running (d). This shows him our app's home screen with the selection of contacts (e). He taps "Pete," and the phone shifts to the connection screen. Only now can he start talking (f).

Now that we've laid it out on a storyboard, we see that launching this app as a classic smartphone app imposes a high overhead compared to the Nextel devices that our customers miss. The smartphone is capable of doing so much more than the Nextel was—playing music, taking photographs, whatever. But precisely because of its wide capabilities, undertaking any particular task means that we have to start by telling the phone which of its many capabilities we want to use. Talking to Pete now requires at least three actions: press the phone's button to turn it on, swipe to unlock, and tap the desired contact. And if our walkie-talkie app isn't the current one, that is, if we've done anything else with our smartphone since the last call (there are some dandy three-D level apps), we'll need additional taps to get to our walkie-talkie app—at least two (tap home, then tap ours)—and maybe a few sideswipes if our walkie-talkie app isn't on the current home page panel. Our user effort has gone from one button press to at least three, and maybe five or more. That's not going to please our users.

The Nextel phone had a hardware button dedicated to this particular task. Talking to Pete used to take just one button press. If we really want to optimize our walkie-talkie app, we'll need to connect to a hardware button in some way. Most modern smartphones, however, do not have dedicated hardware buttons that we can assign to this task. What can we do?

We can buy a dedicated hardware button as an add-on. For example, Pressy (www.pressybutton.com) makes one for Android only. It plugs into the headphone port (Figure 3.13) and triggers a command when you press it. Pressy can recognize sequences of presses as well, perhaps press once for everybody, twice for redial, three times to open the app to the selection page. It's cheap, 15 bucks a pop. You can't use your headphones with it plugged in, but contractors shouldn't be wearing headphones on the job anyway. The storyboard now looks like Figure 3.14.

Pressy isn't the only choice for a hardware button. The Cliq smartphone case has three hardware buttons, which use the NFC chip to communicate with the phone. You can program one action for each button. Unfortunately, Cliq works only if the phone is already on, unless you root it. Another solution could be QuickClick, an app that uses the phone's volume control buttons to launch actions, such as our walkie-talkie app. Which would our users prefer?

We have, through our mockups and storyboards, identified a major stumbling block, that our smartphone app, launched from the home screen, would lose the fundamental benefit of the walkie-talkie: very quick connections to a small set of frequent contacts. We've therefore

Figure 3.13 Pressy add-on button for use with the walkie-talkie app. (Courtesy PressyButton)

Todd's Phone

Figure 3.14 Storyboard of a button with the walkie-talkie app.

uncovered the need for hardware buttons. But no one seems to make an add-on button for the iPhone, at least not at the time of this writing. Our design decision to support hardware buttons in turn leads to the question of whether to support only Android or try to do the iPhone as well. I'd guess that the rough-and-tumble world of the contractor is better suited to Android; we could choose a phone ruggedized to take the pounding, or cheaper for replacement when it breaks. But as always, our users will tell us, once we figure out how to ask them.

As always, the point of this example is not that it is perfect; it isn't. The point is that with this rough cut we have conveyed an amazing amount of information. We can very easily show these choices to our users or their representatives. Which one do you think they'd prefer? They'll understand quickly, and their choices will be clear. We're not polishing a cannonball here.

Demonstrating through Live Action

The storyboards convey a great amount of information with their comic-strip displays. But suppose we wanted to demonstrate the storyboard in a more evocative way. Balsamiq provides a full-screen presentation mode that allows us to demonstrate actual transitions.

On most, but not all, controls, Balsamiq provides a property called Link. This allows you to specify that clicking on that control, while in full-screen presentation mode, switches to another mockup.

Suppose we wanted to show that. Figure 3.15 illustrates what we would do. On the Picture Buttons mockup, we select Pete's button group. The properties of that group appear on the right.

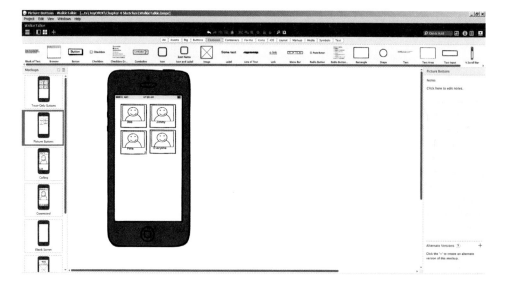

Figure 3.15   Selecting a link for full-screen presentation mode.

Figure 3.16   In full-screen presentation mode.

Clicking on the Link property, we see the list of other mockups. We select the mockup to which we want to transition when the user clicks "Pete." In this case, we select Calling.

Now we can run the full-screen presentation mode by pressing F5. This leads us to Figure 3.16. The mockup is shown on the full screen. The Pete button is shown in pink, indicating that it has a link. When we move the cursor to this button, it changes to a hand, showing the name of the mockup to which it would change if we clicked there. (If we don't like the big cursor or the pink link hint, we can turn them off on the Settings control at the upper right.)

We can continue here, putting in links to show as much of the interaction as we care to. We would probably put a link on the Cancel button to go back to the Picture Buttons mockup and do the same on the Connected screen. To illustrate the transition from the Connecting screen to the Connected screen, we might like to automatically advance after a small delay. This is something that Balsamiq doesn't do. Being a geek, you may be tempted to hack it to try to make it do so, or even to agitate for Balsamiq to add this feature. But consider the simplicity of the interaction that you have had with Balsamiq so far. By adhering to the 80-20 rule, Balsamiq has made everyone's interaction simpler. The whole reason that you are using Balsamiq instead of Visual Studio or Expression Blend is for this simplicity, and its concomitant lower effort and quick turnaround. It is absolutely key to the philosophy. So swallow it, and stop being such a geek.

Now that we have our mockups, we can present them to users as storyboards, which will get us a great deal of information. But if we really want to get good data, we have to test them in action. That's the topic of our next chapter.

CHAPTER 4

TESTING ON LIVE USERS

No matter how good you get at designing user experiences, you will never know how users will react until you test your designs on them. As you have to constantly test the functionality of your code throughout the development process, so you have to constantly test the usability of your program throughout the development process.

Fortunately, doing this testing isn't all that hard or all that expensive. But omitting it can be fatal. And the earlier you start, by far the better. This chapter explains what you need to do.

Testing Constantly, Testing Throughout

"I am the wisest of all men, for I know nothing at all, except that I know nothing at all." That quote is popularly attributed to Socrates, though no one really knows. It's true, though. Probably the biggest shock to my psyche once I started doing this UX gig was this realization: No matter how hard I tried, I could never completely put myself into my users' shoes. I got better at it with experience, as will you. But I now realize that I will never pluck from inside my own mind, nor will you, exactly what our users will understand and enjoy and find helpful and (ideally) buy. Our users are nurses, commuters, cancer patients, auto mechanics, middle-school babysitters. We are, by definition, burned-out computer geeks. Their shoes are just too different from ours for us to imagine a correct fit.

Does that mean that we're screwed no matter what we do? On the contrary. Because we are wise enough to know that we don't know, we are (ideally) wise enough to go and find out. And we are wise enough to know that the only way to find out is to try our designs on actual users. By testing on users, we can see what we've gotten right and what we've gotten wrong, what we've managed to grok correctly and what we're still clueless about. We can then improve our designs based on this new knowledge and repeat the process until we get close enough to make money. It's not that difficult.

Look at the evolution of the case study apps in Chapters 8 and 9, and the additional case studies on this book's Web site. You can see that I started off with some ideas as to how the UX ought to work. But as soon as I showed them to users, I found that (a) things that I thought would make sense to the users didn't make sense, and (b) the users had ideas and needs that had never occurred to me.

As we discussed in the previous chapter, our first design sketches aren't intended to be definitive. They are meant to provoke, to incite, to stir the pot; to dredge ideas out of the users' heads that they never knew that they knew. To encourage them to say, "No, not [this]. But now that you mention it, how about maybe some of [that]?" As we'll see, we can get this done quite well, pretty quickly, and not too expensively.

> ### note
> You will see in this chapter a number of ideas that I have developed starting from Steve Krug's book on usability testing, *Rocket Surgery Made Easy* (New Riders, 2009). If you think you see his influence in this chapter, you are correct.

Why Isn't Testing Done?

Whenever I encounter a UX that sucks like a vacuum cleaner, I inevitably find that it wasn't tested properly for usability. Sometimes it wasn't tested on the right people, or with them doing the right tasks. Once in a while it was tested too late in the development process, so there wasn't time to correct the problems that the testers discovered. But most often, a UX sucks because it was never tested at all. How is this possible?

At first, this seems ludicrous. You wouldn't ship code you hadn't tested and expect it to work correctly, would you? (Don't answer that.) You wouldn't expect your users to be the final debuggers of your functionality, would you? (Ditto.) So how on earth can you possibly ship a UX design that you've never tried on actual users and expect it to work for them? You can't, and if you are wise, you won't. But this happens all the time, and far too many designers (and worse, managers) don't see a problem with that.

Why? Three reasons.

First, too many developers and managers fail to recognize their own fallibility. Here's a quote from Jared Spool's book *Web Site Usability: A Designer's Guide* (Morgan Kaufmann, 1998):

> I had a recent experience with a designer who was invited to observe users of a large commercial real estate site that she had designed. She declined, saying, "I have no need to know what people think of the design. I designed it with a specific purpose in mind, and I believe that I achieved my goal. What could I learn?"
>
> What arrogance! Well, guess what, folks? The users testing the site found it confusing, hard to navigate, difficult to search, and therefore not something they'd be likely to use. I guess if her purpose was to drive people to better sites, she succeeded.

That designer didn't know what she didn't know. She was unwise in the extreme. But you, dear reader, having gotten this far into this book, understand that your user is not you. You know that it doesn't matter a damn what you think, that it only matters what your users think. And by now you've at least started to absorb the notion that you can find out what your users think only by getting that information from them, either via lab testing (this chapter) or via telemetry (next chapter). So this arrogance, born from ignorance of our own ignorance, will not affect us, now will it?

The second reason that UX is not tested is that doing so is perceived as expensive and difficult. Too many developers and managers think you need a full UX testing lab, with one-way glass and lots of special equipment (Figure 4.1). "It's too expensive," they say. "We can't afford it, it's beyond what we're able to do here, and we don't have the time anyway. So we won't even try."

Figure 4.1   You don't actually need expensive equipment to get the job done. (Photo © iStock.com/ Latsalomao)

This perception might have been true a decade ago, but it isn't today. The constantly falling price of all technology and the ubiquitous presence of the Internet mean that we don't need a whole lab full of equipment. The 80-20 law applies here, as it does to most things in life. You can get 80% of the value of UX testing with just 20% of the effort, using nothing more than a PC and Skype. If you don't have these, or aren't willing to use them, I can't help you.

But the biggest obstacle to UX testing is the fundamental misperception that it is a separate step in the UX process. It's not perceived as an ongoing part of an integrated whole. Further, the word *test* seems to indicate that it should get done near the end of the development process (as final code testing is), while exactly the opposite is true.

Compare UX development to the process of writing a book. You start with some ideas jotted on the back of an envelope. Then you bat them around with some people you are comfortable with and refine them—"Hey, did you ever think of [this]?" Based on their comments, you add some items, delete a few, maybe move some around, and come up with an outline, for which you also get feedback. You write a few sample sections, maybe a whole chapter, always, *always* asking for feedback from potential readers as you progress. As Vladimir Nabokov (1899–1977, author of *Lolita*) said, "I have rewritten—often several times—every word I have ever published. My pencils outlast their erasers." If he can't get things right the first time, do you seriously think that you will?

For example, I showed every chapter of *Why Software Sucks* to civilian users, such as my barber, to make sure they could understand it. Here's one true exchange:

Me (in an early draft of *Why Software Sucks*): "The average application programmer knows nothing about what users want."

My barber: What's an application programmer?

Me: Er, application programmers design the front end of programs, while system programmers design the back end.

My barber: WTF?

Me: How about, "The average programmer knows nothing about what users want."

My barber: Why didn't you say so?

Without realizing it, I had used jargon that wasn't part of my readers' world. The difference between an application programmer and a system programmer was part of my everyday vocabulary, but not part of hers. And it's not her job to become "computer literate" to understand terms like these. It was my job to write with words she understood. I couldn't know which ones she did or didn't understand until I asked her. Repeatedly, iteratively, testing your UX on actual users is an integral part of the ongoing UX development process, as editing and rewriting are an integral part of the ongoing book-writing process.

Sketch, test, improve the sketch, test again, improve the sketch, and maybe add some more fidelity, and so on. Don't consider it as a separate, get-the-damn-thing-over-with step in the process. Consider it as one of the ongoing facets of the development process.

One could therefore argue that Chapters 3 (sketching) and 4 (testing) should be merged. But they're different enough in most developers' thoughts today that it makes sense to keep them separate in this volume. I wouldn't be surprised to merge them in the next edition.

CONSULTING CLIENTS

It is sometimes hard to convince customers that they should pay for usability testing. They see that line item and say, "What? You want us to pay you to find and fix your own mistakes?! Big negatory on that one, my friend." That's another reason not to single it out as a separate stage. It's just part of your regular iterative UX development process, as editing is a part of all writing. Call it "our ongoing UX quality review, in accordance with the very best practices," if that's what you need to get it approved.

Above all, remember this question and its answer: What is the best kind of UX test? Like seat belts or birth control, it's the one that you actually use, rather than the one you sit around and think about and say, "That would have been good, but damn, we're out of time. Maybe for our next project."

Start Testing Early

If you've ever done any navigation, you know that the earlier you apply a course correction, the smaller the correction you need to make, and the lower the cost of that correction in time and fuel and aggravation. For some reason, this obvious notion has never gotten far in the UX design process. The second-biggest mistake anyone ever makes in UX testing (after not doing it at all) is starting it too late in the development process.

Microsoft likes to say, "We eat our own dog food," meaning that they use their own programs internally before releasing them to customers. This is way too late for usability testing, because it's way too late to change anything. The development has been done, the budgets spent, the attitudes hardened. You need to do better.

But how can we test the UX if it's not finished? The answer is with the low-fidelity mockups you saw in the previous chapter. You start with the least detailed, sketchiest design and refine it as you get user feedback. "All this stuff together is too cramped; you can't pick things out of it." "OK, we'll spread it out some, think about the relative importance of each item, maybe put some on different tabs. Here's a quick example. Now what do you think?" And so on.

In addition to starting your testing early, you need to conduct it often. Krug recommends once per month, always at the same time (the morning of the third Thursday, or whatever). That way your devs know when it's going to be and can plan around it. And the deadline will encourage them to make their features ready by then. For a system that is more or less in a steady state, such as Beth Israel Deaconess Medical Center's PatientSite (see Chapter 9) once it got rolled out, this is a good frequency. However, when you are in active development, as many of my clients are, with tight deadlines, test usability more frequently. Run testing sessions at least weekly, possibly more often as you work up your designs. That keeps you from wasting time in blind alleys.

What We Learn from UX Testing

This laboratory testing of our UX complements the telemetry discussed in Chapter 5. Telemetry has a wider reach, since we can instrument our entire program. It can record data from large numbers of users. But there are two critical things that only human-on-human lab testing can do for us.

First, we can't use telemetry until we have some sort of working software to put in front of our users. The biggest advantage of laboratory testing is that we can start it as soon as we have even scratches on the back of a napkin. As I just explained, the earlier you make a correction, the less it costs. UX testing gives us the earliest indications of how users are going to react to our programs. They like this. They don't like that. Such-and-such is good once they find it, but they have trouble finding it, and so on. This early feedback is probably the biggest advantage of live usability testing.

The second advantage of UX testing is that we can discuss their feelings with our actual users. Telemetry could tell us, say, that 80% of users cancel dialog box A, whereas 20% of users cancel dialog box B. But only live users can tell us what they were actually thinking when they did this. Did they get to box A by mistake? What did they think that box A was going to do for them? What caused them to click Cancel rather than OK?

As they use our mockups during the test, we ask them to think out loud. This stream of consciousness contains important information: "I came here to do this; I'm looking for where it is. Here? No, that's something else. Maybe here? That looks like it makes more sense. Not here either. Damn, where'd they put it?" And so on. We can also ask them questions about their interaction at the end of the test: "Did you see this over here? What do you think it might do?" We can't get this information any other way. And again, having this insight early in the development process guides our steps and keeps us focused on the users' actual needs and wants.

Finding Test Users

When you test your application's usability, you need your test subjects to be as similar to your real users as you possibly can. It's tempting just to show it to the people in your development shop and ask what they think. But there is no quicker road to hell than doing this. Who is your user not? You. And probably not your coworkers, either.

The types of test users and relationships that you will need depend on the type of development that you are doing. Here are some cases you might have to deal with:

Suppose you are writing customized software for a company to use in-house. We call this a "line-of-business application." Users spend a lot of time using it, often all day, every day, and their success in their business depends on its functionality. Imagine, for example, a policy administration app for use by an insurance company's customer service reps. You might be developing this system as part of an in-house development team, or perhaps as an outside consulting company. (I've seen plenty of both.)

Your development team needs to have good relations with these users. They're the ones who are going to be stuck with this app. Their success is your success, and their failure is yours as well. They're the ones whose productivity and comfort level are paramount.

You don't always have a working relationship with them at the start of a project. Sometimes the target users' supervisor, overworked like everyone these days, won't allow them to take time from their workday to talk to you. That's shortsighted. Sometimes the users don't believe that good UX is even possible. They've had garbage shoved down their throats way too many times. They don't realize that their participation is valuable, nay, essential, to the process. "Wait a minute, you're the expert. Can't you just go write your program without bothering me?" The answer is "No, not if it's going to be any good." The first deliverable will often start changing their minds: "Hey, it doesn't suck as badly as the previous one. Do you think we could maybe . . . ?" When they see their requests actually listened to and implemented, and their working lives made easier because of it, they will become your staunchest allies.

The one thing you have to be *extremely* careful of in this type of situation is to avoid excessive dependency on the technophile user. "We need someone to be our liaison to the development team." "Oh, get Bob, he's the computer guy." If you get a volunteer, it's often because that guy is interested in technology, likes technology, wants to work with technology. He probably doesn't realize that the rest of the users aren't like him. (Or perhaps if he does realize that, he doesn't care, or perhaps even revels in his self-perceived superiority.) These technophiles are not usually your primary target audience.[1] You have to be very careful not to let his technophilic ideas override the need to please the larger user population—not nearly as technophilic as Bob, because they didn't volunteer. In this case, perhaps keep Bob as your contact for day-to-day matters. He may do a better job of responding to phone calls and emails because he's interested. But when you do the usability testing sessions, rotate the testing role over all of the users in the group. That way everyone feels listened to, and no particular ideology dominates.

Consider another case: You are building a system for external business clients. Continuing the previous example, suppose our insurance company now wants a Web application for independent insurance agents to use in accessing their customers' policies. The easier that Web application is to use, the more the independent agents will favor your company over others for which access is more difficult. Again, the application could be built by an independent consulting company, or by the carrier's in-house staff. How would you handle user representation in this case?

Ideally you would recruit one of the targeted insurance agencies to be your launch partner, as Boeing chooses an airline to be the launch customer airline for a new airplane. (Remember Pan Am and the first 747, or All Nippon Airways on the 787?) You would treat this launch customer as if they were in-house users—actually better than if they were in-house users, because you can't cram things down their throats. You'd have a liaison at the target customer, sometimes called the product owner. You'd run the tests on rotating members of the user population.

Finally we come to the case of software built for individual consumers. To test this, you need to recruit individual users. It's a lot easier to snag users for testing than it used to be. Not so long ago, you needed to have a fully instrumented UX testing lab with one-way glass so you could watch users struggle with your creations. You had to convince them to come to your lab and then transport them there, and then home when you were finished. It took much more of their time, thereby skewing your user selection toward seniors and the unemployed.

With today's ubiquitous Internet connectivity, you can perform your testing wherever the users congregate. To get mall shoppers, you'd set up in a mall. To get seniors, you'd go to a

---

1. See my article "The Silent Majority: Why VB6 Still Thrives" in the June 2012 edition of *MSDN Magazine* for more discussion of this issue.

senior center. Commuter rail riders? The commuter rail station. Students? Their school. Library patrons? (You get the idea.) You do your testing right there in their native habitat.

How many users do you need? Surprisingly few. Steve Krug says three. Jakob Nielsen says five to eight. In general, I'm in the three camp. I'd rather have three test runs with three users each than two runs with five users. I figure that if three out of three users think something is pretty good, it probably is. If zero out of three users can figure something out, your app is seriously messed up. If one out of three is OK with it, it's probably still bad, but fix the zeros first. On the other hand, once you've gone to the trouble to send your moderator to an external site and set up, if you can get five users through the test, you might as well do so.

Above all, start soon. Don't let the search for the perfect users blind you to the good-enough users. Time is your enemy.

Compensating Test Users

You need to compensate your test users for participating in your test. Exactly what form this compensation takes depends on the situation. It does not need to be large, but it does need to be immediate. "Your gift will arrive in four to six weeks" doesn't cut it.

Something related to the business for which you are developing the software is probably a good place to start. If you're testing a movie ticket purchasing app on movie theater patrons, how about some free movie passes? Or maybe refreshment vouchers, so they can enjoy them immediately. If you're testing an order-ahead app for a gourmet food store, how about a gift card for that store? If you're testing at a health club, how about an extra month of free membership? The cost of this reward is tiny compared to the time and effort of your people who are running the test, and exactly zero compared to the value of what you are learning from it. If you can't think of anything better, a crisp new $20 bill always crinkles nicely.

If you're in an in-house situation where cash or gifts are inappropriate, an order-in lunch for the volunteers usually gets the job done. If you're recruiting test users at a nonprofit outfit such as a school, perhaps offer a donation to that institution: "We'll donate $50 to the school for every user who stops by Room 303 to try our new software." Make sure you hand the principal a check before you leave for the day, with attendant photos and publicity.

Test Area Design and Setup

Ideally you want the test area to mimic the area in which users will be using the software. If it's for, say, bartenders in crowded restaurants, you won't get valid results by doing the test in a quiet office. Taking your test to where the users are will help you get accurate results.

You will need to watch your users' actions live. So hook up the testing environment with Camtasia or GoToMeeting software, or whatever other products best suit your needs. You want to see the exact usage patterns of the users as they perform their tasks. Do they, for example, move the mouse to the left first, before realizing that the control they need is on the right? And so on.

Train a camera on the users while they use the software. Their body language and facial expressions convey important information. Videos of the most vivid reactions—a user jumping for joy when using a good app, or sticking her finger down her throat when using a bad one—are just the sorts of things you need to sell your management on the efficacy of your testing and your entire UX effort.

On the other hand, the camera could conceivably make them self-conscious and change the data you collect. Start with it on and see what you get, and if you have to turn it off, then do.

Using a Moderator

You need a team member to handle the test users—to bring them in, to settle them down, to explain the test, to assist them as they go through it, then to ask questions at the end. To mediate between the development team, with its geeky attitude, and the all-too-human test users. In theatrical parlance, this person is sometimes called a "wrangler," but in this context we'll use the term *moderator*.

A usability test moderator requires a different skill set from that of most software geeks. A moderator needs empathy, the ability to relate to humans, to put them at their ease. You will find out fairly quickly who at your company is good at it and who isn't. Call me a sexist, but I've found that the good ones are female more often than male.

The moderator welcomes the users into the test environment and makes sure they are comfortable. Bathroom? Coffee? Donut? Sure. The moderator walks each user through any paperwork, such as the release document that your legal department will probably require in case your app is so bad that the test user chokes on the donut and dies during your test.

The moderator then explains the testing process to the user. Most books recommend doing this by reading a prepared script, thereby removing a possible source of variability. This book does not include a script, but you can find plenty of them with a quick Google search. You will probably modify them at least somewhat for your particular setup.

The script explains to the users that we aren't testing them. They can't make a mistake. We're testing our software, to see how good a job *we* have done in making the software easy for them. The most important thing that the users can do is to think aloud as they're performing their task: "Where's the login screen? Oh, there it is. What, it doesn't like my password? Phooey." And so on. It's often good to remind the users, "Don't worry about hurting our feelings. We need to find out what our users really think. Besides, we're engineers; we don't have any feelings."

The moderator ideally sits behind the user during a test, doing her best to remove herself from the user's consciousness, but off to the side a little so she can still see the screen. Ideally the moderator stays silent, though this is not always possible. The most important data comes from the user's stream of consciousness, so encouragement to think out loud is important. The moderator will often need to say things like "What are you thinking now? Can you tell me more? Thank you, that's great, that's exactly the sort of thing we're looking to hear from you."

Sometimes users will get stuck. You wish they wouldn't, you try to write the software so they don't, but it happens. The moderator ideally waits for the user to say something like "I'm stuck." Then the moderator says, "What do you think might work?" "Well, maybe [this]." "Why don't you try [this] and see what it does?" Again, you will quickly find who has the knack to be a good moderator.

Task Design and Description

You can't get any useful data from just asking users to "try our site and tell us how you like it." You have to give them an objective, a specific task, such as "Check the flights from Boston to Tallahassee next week. Buy the lowest-cost flight leaving on Tuesday morning and returning on Thursday after work." Make sure that the users have whatever supporting items they will need, for example, a user ID/password pair when login is required, or perhaps a credit card for simulated purchases.

You need to describe the task in terms of the user's mental model rather than the site's implementation model. Jared Spool writes of a test that he once did for Ikea.com. Ikea's Web designers had told their test users to "find a bookcase." Not surprisingly, all the users typed "bookcase" into the site's search box and found it quickly. But when Spool told users, "You have 200-plus books in your fiction collection. Find a way to organize them," the users behaved very differently. They browsed the site's aisles instead of using the search box. And when they did search, it wasn't for the term *bookcase*, it was for *shelves*.

Obviously, the task and the setup will vary from one application or site to another. You need to focus very carefully on exactly what you want to measure. Consider the popular music site Pandora.com, shown in Figure 4.2. The biggest problem any Web site has is explaining itself to the viewer in the second or two that the user is willing to invest before saying, "Hell with this. Too much work," and jumping somewhere else. Imagine that the users don't know what Pandora's about. The key to hooking the new users is not to make them think ("Click here to create an account"), but to start catering to them—in this case, playing music that they like. The moderator might simply say, "Start playing some music," or perhaps "Start playing some music that you like." The user will quickly see that there's only one thing to do. This very easy entry is one of the reasons that Pandora is as successful as it is.

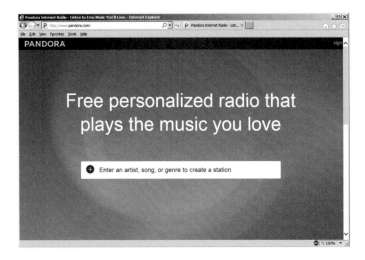

Figure 4.2   Pandora.com initial screen. It is very easy for a user to figure out.

Watching and Debriefing

You will definitely want some of your usability staff to watch the test live. They will see user actions that they've never thought of before. These in turn will suggest questions that they might want to ask the users. And the major advantage of in-person testing over telemetry is that you can ask those questions while the users still remember what they did and why.

It is also a very good idea to have some non-UX developers watch this interaction to start gaining at least some understanding of the users that they're ultimately working for and need to satisfy. You will have to get management buy-in for the developers to take time off from their tasks to observe this. But a rotating schedule, so that each developer observes perhaps once every month or two, is an affordable balance. It won't take much avoidance of blind alleys to repay that amount of time. If they are reluctant, bribe them with food.

It's important that they watch the actual user interaction, not just the debriefing afterward. As Alan Cooper writes in *About Face* (Wiley, 2014), "[Usability professionals] drag programmers into dark rooms, where they watch through one-way mirrors as hapless users struggle with their software. At first, the programmers suspect that the test subject has brain damage. Finally, after much painful observation, the programmers are forced to bow to empirical evidence. They admit that their user interface design needs work, and they vow to fix it."

Today you don't even need a one-way mirror. So there's no excuse not to test.

Sometimes the users enjoy meeting the developers; more commonly they don't. The developers are sort of like surgeons, technicians who chose their profession because they don't like talking to people. But sometimes the back-and-forth interaction can be useful, especially under the soothing (for both sides) influence of the moderator. For example:

> **Moderator:** "Did you see [this button]?"
>
> **User:** "Yes."

The developers will want to scream, "Then why didn't you click it, you idiot?" The moderator needs to translate that into something that the user finds inoffensive, probably something based on the program as an actor rather than the user. For example, "What did you think it might do?" or better, "What was it saying to you?" Then maybe a follow-up: "Actually that button activated the checkout process [or whatever]. Go ahead and click it now. [User does so.] We sure didn't explain that well, did we? [No, you sure didn't.] What could we have said that would have made it clear what this would do for you?" And so on.

At the end of the test run, your project team members have had their noses rubbed in their failings. It's vital to grab them while they still have the smell in their nostrils. You need an immediate debriefing session, before they have time to concoct rationalizations and excuses: "Well, you obviously recruited these users from a mental institution. Let me have a chance to put them through training first." No. We're going to fix our UX.

You need to identify the root causes of the failures—failures, again, of *your* design, not of the users. Things like "The monthly pass link was off on the side, and the user couldn't see it. And the label said 'perpetual,' not 'renewal,' which not one single user understood."

You need to assign each identified problem to a specific person. That person is then responsible to investigate and return within 24 hours with recommendations for a solution.

User Testing Example

To demonstrate an actual usability test for this chapter, we'll use Balsamiq to create a mockup of the PC player program provided by Live365.com (Figure 4.3). Started in 1999, Live365 was one of the first music broadcast stations on the Internet. Like so many bold Internet pioneers (anyone remember pets.com?), Live365 couldn't adapt to today's world, but it struggled long and valiantly. In fact, Live365 went belly up in early 2016, just as this book was entering its final editing stage. I decided to keep this section in the book as a salute to this trailblazer, from which I derived many hours of musical enjoyment.

As we'll see, their UX definitely needed improvement. The lessons that we'll learn from studying it come too late for Live365, but they might just save *your* butt, dear reader.

Figure 4.3 Live365 PC player.

Anyone wanting to broadcast an audio program could upload content to Live365 and stream it to listeners anywhere on the Internet. Some broadcasters were hobbyists who enjoyed playing DJ, some were bands promoting their own music, some were airwave radio stations simulcasting their signal, and some were pure Internet stations. Live365 made money by charging broadcasters, from $5 per month for the most basic package up to $200 per month for professionals.

Listeners could tune in free with ads, or buy an ad-free VIP subscription for $5 per month. They could use a Web browser or player apps for various devices. A listener could choose from many streams but had no choice as to the contents of that stream. That was entirely up to the broadcasters. Listeners could send likes or dislikes to the DJ through the player app, but they couldn't skip songs. If you think of Live365 as Songza without skipping, you'll have the right mental model of the listening experience.

Why, then, if you couldn't skip songs you disliked, would you have listened to Live365 instead of Pandora or Songza? The answer is: Since Live365 allowed anyone to broadcast a stream, listeners had a huge number of streams to choose from. Songza touts the quality of its curated streams. Live365 figured that among its very large quantity, you'd find something you like. I enjoy Songza's curated streams. But they don't have much of the beach music/surf rock that I enjoy. Live365 had five or six such streams, with the various creative viewpoints of their DJs. So I found myself listening to all these music sites depending on my cranky mood.

I often stream music at my PC when I'm working. I could stream it in a browser, but I prefer the dedicated player app shown previously. Live365 clearly considered this player an extra benefit, because unlike the apps for mobile devices, you could get the PC player only if you paid your VIP membership fee. The PC player had some UX deficiencies when examined by current standards, so we want to test it on some users.

Where should these test users come from? As always, we need to ask who the target market is for our software. Live365 touted the PC player as a bonus to entice ordinary members to upgrade. So our target users should ideally consist of ordinary Live365 members. If this player could have made them happier, maybe more of them would have upgraded, and maybe Live365 might still be around, right?

We could invite users to enroll as test subjects by playing a commercial in their non-VIP audio streams, offering a reward for their participation. What kind of prize should we offer them? Any user can get a trial VIP membership for free, but it lasts only five days. How about offering them a free three-month VIP membership for participating in our usability tests? We'd get test subjects, and maybe they'd get addicted to the lack of commercials and sign up when the free trial was over.

Since I've never been affiliated with Live365 in any way, and therefore didn't have access to its subscribers, I fell back on my trusty all-purpose user population, otherwise known as my daughters. They stream music a lot, from a number of sources. And you *know* they're not shy about stating their likes and dislikes. (I wonder where they get that from?) I brought them into my testing lab, one at a time, and ran the following session. Imagine that the paperwork has all been done and the user is ready. Here's how one session went:

> **Moderator:** Are you good to go ?
>
> **Subject:** Sure.
>
> **Moderator:** OK, I'm going to launch the Live365 player for you. Here it is. [Launches player mockup from F5 in Balsamiq; see Figure 4.4. Also launches music stream in the background, playing through the PC speakers, so it feels like the Balsamiq mockup is actually playing.] See it OK?
>
> **Subject:** Sure.
>
> **Moderator:** How do you like this song?
>
> **Subject:** It's pretty good.
>
> **Moderator:** Imagine you really like this song. And you want to somehow tell the DJ about it, so he would play this song and others like it more often. What would you do?
>
> **Subject:** I'd click Like on the player.

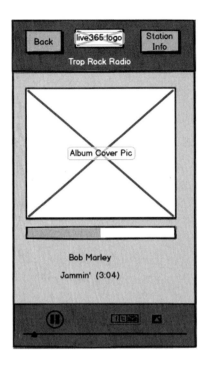

Figure 4.4   Initial Balsamiq display of Live365 PC player mockup.

Moderator: Why don't you go ahead and do that? And remember, as I asked you earlier: it would really help us if you could think out loud while you do it.

Subject: OK. Where's the Like button? I don't see one. Does it even have one? Hmmm . . . [falls silent]

Moderator: Could you tell us what you're thinking now please?

Subject: OK. Looking at the top, no; middle, no; bottom. Where's the Like button? Is that a tiny little Facebook thing I see there?

Moderator: What do you think?

Subject: It looks like Facebook. But it's gray. Does that mean it doesn't work? What would happen if I clicked it?

Moderator: Why don't you give it a try?

Subject: Now I get Facebook and Twitter and Email buttons on my player [Figure 4.5]. That's surprising. I thought I'd go straight to Facebook from clicking that, but I guess it just brought up these choices. I'll try Facebook now . . . [mockup Facebook page opens; see Figure 4.6]

Subject: It looks like this goes to my own Facebook. I don't want to be in Facebook. I just want to like the damn song. OK, I'll close Facebook. I'm back at the same place I was before.

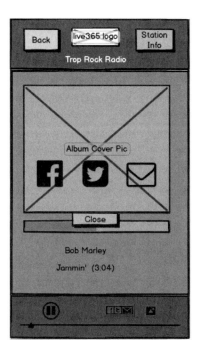

Figure 4.5 PC player after clicking the Share button.

Figure 4.6 Mockup after the user selects Facebook for sharing.

I'm still not seeing a Like button. Songza has a Like button. What's wrong with this stupid thing?

Moderator (momentarily considers saying, "Because they're a bunch of idiots, that's why"; throttles the impulse and remains intentionally silent)

Subject: Let's see, there's this other little thing here. Some sort of triangle. No indication about what it does, but that's about all there is to click on. Might as well try it. Ah, there's something. [screen labeled "Other" comes up; see Figure 4.7] Where's the Like button? I'm not seeing it. There, that one says "Like." Why does it have a check mark instead of a thumbs up? It's probably the same thing. I'll click that. There, that seems to have done it.

Moderator: OK, thank you. You've successfully sent your like to the DJ. Just a couple of questions before we finish. Tell me, what do you think of this way of sending likes and dislikes?

Subject: I don't like it at all. First, the buttons should be obvious, and these aren't. I mean, it didn't take me that long to find them, but I shouldn't have had to dig around at all. They're hidden. Why do they do that?

Moderator: I don't know, but I'll definitely pass that along. What else are you thinking?

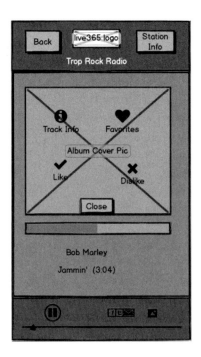

Figure 4.7   Live365 mockup labeled "Other." This is where the Like and Dislike buttons are hidden.

Subject: After I found where they'd hidden the Like button, it takes two clicks for me to send a like or dislike, every single time. I'm barely willing to make the effort to click once on a Like button. Two clicks is more work than I'm willing to do. And the check mark and X symbols? Why don't they use thumbs up and thumbs down like everyone else?

Moderator: Darned if I know either. I'll tell them about it. Here's your allowance, now go out and play.

Now imagine that we're at the debriefing. The second test user (my other daughter) did and said pretty much what the first user did. Let's consider what we learned from this test. We found the following problems:

- Subject had to search to find Like/Dislike buttons.
- Subject did not initially recognize Like/Dislike buttons.
- Subject had to click twice to send Like/Dislike message.

All three problems are obviously connected. One person should be assigned to research these problems and recommend solutions within the next 24 hours. Here are some things we might try:

How about putting Like and Dislike buttons on the player screen? I know of no other player with Like/Dislike buttons that buries them this way. If the user's likes and dislikes are important, the buttons should be easier to access. Did Live365 deliberately make them harder to access? Have we decided, as a matter of policy, that we want to hear from the user only if he feels strongly enough about liking or disliking to go through the effort of clicking twice? I don't think we are, but if I'm wrong, let's discuss it now. And while we're at it, let's change the icons to the thumbs up and thumbs down that other sites use. We don't have the volume to buck Facebook's and Google's standards as to what icons mean. And as long as we're moving to standard icons, how about the Share icon? It can still lead to the selection screen in Figure 4.5, but why not use the standard one?

Where should these buttons go? Space is tight in the PC player window. Does the volume slider really need all the space that it's taking up, side to side at the bottom of the screen? YouTube uses a small speaker icon that expands when the user hovers on it and then shrinks back down when the user moves away. Let's switch to that now. Besides saving space, it communicates better. Users are sometimes confused between the volume slider at the bottom and the progress bar right under the album.

Now that we've moved the Like/Dislike buttons off the Other screen shown in Figure 4.7, what are we left with? Only the Track Info button and the Favorites button. The Track Info button emails the user information about the currently playing title and artist, with links in the email from which the user can purchase the track. Email? Links? How twentieth century. If there's one thing mobile apps are about, it's enabling easy purchases. How about changing this to a purchase button and moving that to the main screen as well?

So now we're left with the Favorites button, which adds the station to the user's Favorites list if it's not already there, or removes it if it is. Having a separate screen just for this is wasteful. How about a star on the screen, or maybe a heart, outlined to indicate unselected and filled to indicate selected? Since it applies to the station, not the track, how about putting it at the top, near the Station Info button, or maybe the name?

Figure 4.8 shows the mockup modified based on these ideas, all stemming from this simple usability test. We put the icons having to do with playing the music, the play/pause and the volume, together on the left. We put the icons having to do with liking the music, the thumbs up and down, on the right. The sharing icon, telling other people about the track, went along with these. Buying the track went along with liking it, so the shopping cart went next to the thumbs up. We put the star, for favorites, up near the top.

Of course more research is needed; it always is. But we've improved this app by a great deal, with fast, cheap testing of low-fidelity mockups on users. We'll test all this at next week's run. Or maybe I can squeeze another one in today, if my daughters aren't too busy.

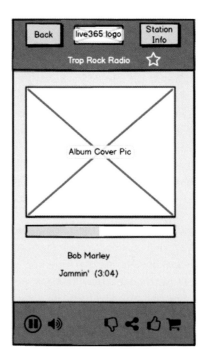

Figure 4.8   Improved Live365 mockup.

The Last Word in Usability Testing

I have always admired Frederick P. Brooks, author of the classic book *The Mythical Man-Month*. His ideas on software architecture and development have valuable lessons to teach us today, even though some of the anecdotes are so old that they describe programs stored on punch cards.

He has written a more recent book, entitled *The Design of Design: Essays from a Computer Scientist* (Addison-Wesley, 2010). It contains an anecdote that resonates with me whenever I start thinking about usability testing, and the need for starting it early. Brooks writes (emphasis mine):

> My team spent some ten years realizing our dream of a "room-filling protein" virtual image. My idea was that the chemists could more readily find their way around in the complex molecule by knowing where the C-end and the N-end were positioned in the physical room. After many disappointments, we finally had a suitable high-resolution image in a head-mounted display. The chemist could readily walk around in the protein structure to study areas of interest.
>
> Our first user came for her biweekly appointment; all went well and she moved about quite a bit. Next session, same thing. Third session: "May I have a chair?" *A decade's work shot down by one sentence!* The navigation assistance wasn't worth the physical labor.

Don't let this happen to you. Test early, test often, and test continually.

CHAPTER 5

TELEMETRY AND ANALYTICS

To really understand our users, we need to see how they use our applications in actual practice—what they actually do, not what they can remember doing, or are willing to admit to doing. Lab testing and interviews provide us only a limited glimpse.

Today's apps, connected over the Internet, can report our users' actual behavior, in all parts of our programs and over very large sample groups. We can then examine usage patterns and behaviors to meet our users' needs. This chapter explains how we can do that.

The Guessing Game Era

I remember frustrating design meetings in the late eighties and early nineties, when we were trying to figure out how users actually did use our program. The discussions would almost always go thusly:

> **First engineer:** Users always do [this].
>
> **Second engineer:** No way. I know users, and they never do [this]. They always do [that]. You're an idiot.
>
> **First engineer:** I'm not an idiot. You're the idiot, you idiot. Users don't do [that], they do [this]. And you're ugly.

When I sat down with either engineer (separately, of course) and forced him to walk me through the reasons why he thought that users did this or that, it invariably boiled down to "because that's what I do." As we've seen throughout this book, your user is not you, and our users weren't either one of those guys either. Through interviews or discreet observation, we would eventually discover that the users did neither this nor that but something completely different, something we'd never expected or planned for and initially couldn't believe.

As we saw in the preceding chapter, observing live users interacting with our programs is immensely valuable. We can talk to the test users. We can ask them why they did this instead of that or the other way around, or if they noticed this thing over here, or what they thought would happen if they did such-and-such. Asking them, "What are you thinking now?" when they appear to be stuck often sheds light on confusing designs.

But this approach has limits. You can test only one or two features at a session, a tiny proportion of most apps. You have a small sample group, which means that one or two atypical users can skew the data. Even with the best of moderators, users are sometimes too polite, or reluctant to appear dumb, or can't remember enough to give you good responses. Researchers often poison the process by asking leading questions. And you are observing only a very short user interaction—first impressions are useful, but they don't measure long-term behavior. You can't test how user interactions evolve over time. Live testing can't answer some vital questions, such as which features users actually use most frequently. And whether your app's more advanced features, such as keyboard shortcuts, are ever getting used at all.

Consider the example from earlier in this book. Microsoft Word requires users to manually save changes to their documents. Microsoft OneNote saves them automatically, unless the user explicitly discards them. Which is better for users?

It depends on how often the users save their changes versus how often they discard them. If users save their changes 99% of the time, then automatic saving would eliminate 95 clicks out of every 100 in the saving process, a huge reduction of overall user effort. On the other hand, if users save their changes only 50% of the time, then automatic saving would actually increase the overall user effort by a lot; every 100 clicks in the saving process would now mushroom to 250.

How do you know what percentage of users save their changes? Not by some mystical telepathic intuition, known only to crystal gazers who burn incense and eat sprouts and wear berets. Even asking a few users in the lab won't tell you. But collecting hard engineering data, over many more users than you could afford to test in the lab, will give you the answers that you need to make the correct decision.

Telemetry as a Solution

To fill in these blank spaces in our knowledge, we need automated, unattended monitoring of users' actions. We need to track all of the users' actions, not just the few we can cram into a one-hour lab session. We need to do it in such a way that our observation process doesn't alter their behavior. We need to collect this data over time, to see how it changes. We need large numbers of users, so we can make statistically valid inferences. And, of course, we need it at the lowest possible cost.

Almost all computers today are connected to the Internet at least sporadically. We can therefore meet these needs by adding code to our programs that records what users do and reports this data to a central server. We can then understand user behavior by examining this data store. We can then make design decisions based on actual user behavior, rather than WAGs (wild-ass guesses).

This process goes by the name of *telemetry and analytics*. In this context, I define telemetry as "the automated collection of data describing user actions in an application." I define analytics as "the study of telemetry data to understand and improve the user experience." In practice, the term is often shortened simply to the catchall term *telemetry*. Figure 5.1 shows the process.

The developer registers her app with the telemetry provider. The app then runs in its native environment, here shown on a mobile device. When the app is connected to the Internet, it sends data describing its actions to the telemetry database run by the provider. If the app is not connected, it logs its information locally until the connection is reestablished. The developer later views the results of the telemetry through the telemetry provider's Web site and makes development decisions based on this data.

Good telemetry data can help you focus your next development cycle. For example, in a mobile device app, how often do your users hold the device in landscape orientation versus portrait orientation? I once saw a conference speaker offer his attendees a game to download and run on their phones while he spoke. At the end of the talk, he showed telemetry data that revealed that 87% of the attendees had held their devices in portrait orientation while running it. That

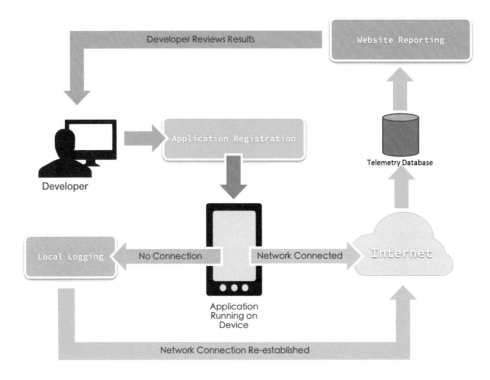

Figure 5.1   Telemetry and analytics process. (Courtesy of Xamarin)

would suggest that further development of landscape mode would probably not be the best use of their limited development dollars.

For another example of the importance of telemetry, consider the A-B test. Suppose you have two versions of an ad. How do you know which is more effective? For, say, a week, you randomly show incoming users either version A or version B and measure which one gets more clicks. A client of mine makes a product related to online safety and gets a lot of customers through Internet ads. He tried two versions. One showed a user relaxing in a hammock and drinking lemonade because the product had done all his work for him. The other showed bad guys trying to do bad things to a user. The product fought them off, but another user, who hadn't bought the product, fell victim. The client and I both favored the former. We both said, "Aw, baloney [we were a little more graphic], who's going to click on a cheesy thing like that other one? I wish I was lying in that hammock now." But the customers clicked on the scary one, by a factor of three or more. We couldn't argue with that data. Our users weren't us.

Good telemetry data can settle arguments with bosses and customers, whereas the lack of it leaves you back in the bad old days. I have a client today whose product displays data in a set of tabs. These tabs are movable, as are the tabs on most Web browsers. This feature probably exists because one specific power user demanded it, but the other users find it more of a bug than a feature—they accidentally displace a tab, don't realize what they did to cause it, and Undo doesn't work to put it back. It seems to be a rather large net negative in the program. If that app had telemetry, I could measure how often tabs get moved into particular configurations, versus how often they're restored to their original locations after being displaced. But I came in late to this project, and it doesn't have telemetry. I can't prove it one way or the other. It's frustrating as heck.

Telemetry is especially important when you are iterating quickly. You make some changes, roll them out, and you can see within a day or two what users are doing, or not doing, with them. You can then adjust and respond for your next release in a week or two. Eric Ries champions this approach in his book *The Lean Startup* (Crown, 2011). With today's ever-shorter release cycles, telemetry is more important than ever.

Evolution of Telemetry

It may seem new, but telemetry has actually been around for years. We first saw it on the earliest Web pages. You probably remember the hit counters that said, "You are visitor number [whatever]." The site owner would see when traffic had gone up or down and could adjust content accordingly. This then evolved to Web server logs showing where Web site users were coming from, the days and times at which they were hitting your site, and so on.

It was easy to do this. Google Analytics, for example, can track the usage of your Web site by means of small scripts that you include on each page. Listing 5.1 shows an excerpt from one such script.

Listing 5.1 Enabling Google Analytics Tracking

```
<script type="text/javascript">
    var pageTracker = _gat._getTracker("UA-1134649-2");
    pageTracker._trackPageview();
</script>
```

When a customer hits the page, the script sends information to Google, which stores it in its massive databases. You can then view various parameters in a browser—the number of hits, the places they came from, the browsers used, and so on (Figure 5.2). It is almost infinitely configurable, to the extent (Google claims) of figuring out the age and gender profile of your visitors.

Reading these entrails was and remains a highly speculative operation. But it's easy and cheap to collect and view this data, so you might as well do it. For example, one of my students once noticed that her company's Web site was receiving a lot of hits from Japan, even though it was written in English. The question, of course, was whether these hits represented actual human users and thus potential customers, or it was just spam spiders working through a Japanese portal. She tried adding a short blurb in Japanese, which attracted many more viewers, and therefore she decided to expand the site's support for Japanese.

That was for Web sites, in which users are by definition always connected to the Internet. Desktop apps are a different story. Around 2007, Microsoft applications started showing the dialog box shown in Figure 5.3. This was Microsoft's first attempt at telemetry for desktop

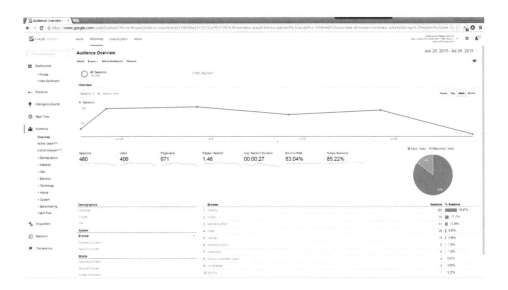

Figure 5.2   Representation of a browser showing Google Analytics data.

Help improve Internet Explorer: Join the Customer Experience Improvement Program

We invite you to join our Customer Experience Improvement Program to help improve the quality, reliability and performance of Internet Explorer.

If you accept, we'll collect anonymous information about your hardware configuration and how you use Internet Explorer to identify trends and usage patterns. We will not collect your name, address, or any other personally identifiable information. This service is completely anonymous.

☐ Participate in the Customer Experience Improvement Program (recommended).

You can stop participating in this program at any time by clicking Help and selecting Customer Feedback Options. For more information about this program, read Internet Explorer's Privacy Statement online.

Figure 5.3   First permission screen for Microsoft CEIP.

applications. The developers had written an internal framework that recorded and forwarded information on user activities. They figured that enough of their customers were connected to the Internet enough of the time that they could get good information about their experiences.

Microsoft was smart enough to give its telemetry program a friendly name, "Customer Experience Improvement Program (CEIP)," as opposed to such earlier missteps as "Hailstorm" and "Carnivore." The company promised anonymity. It politely asked permission and left the check box empty so that users had to opt in to be tracked. This was the first time any company was observing desktop apps on any kind of scale, and Microsoft could have gotten hammered for it. But the company made nice and was rewarded. Now all of its programs, including Windows itself, make extensive use of telemetry.

Today we have mobile devices and their apps. They're connected to the Web almost all the time. Their very utility stems from their connected mobility. They report data to their home bases at times and places that we don't really think about. Consider the traffic features of the Google Maps traffic app (Figure 5.4).

Google's map shows you where you are and what traffic is around you. How does it know the traffic level, magic image recognition from a fleet of drones? Nothing so fancy. Your phone is constantly reporting its location to Google so that Google can show your position on the map. Google knows where you are now, and it knows where you were a minute ago, so it knows how fast you're traveling. It knows which road you're on, and hence what the speed limit is, so it can figure out whether you're cruising along in the green, slogging in yellow, or cursing in red.

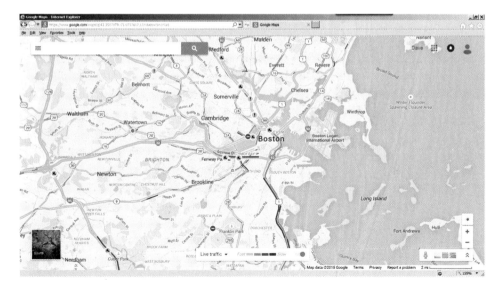

Figure 5.4 Google Maps traffic based on telemetry.

This reporting of data is baked into the application. Here the line starts to blur between an app's primary function and its UX telemetry. That's how today's apps work. We'll discuss this in more detail as we proceed with our exploration.

Permission and Privacy

Your telemetry app is going to be monitoring and reporting on a user's actions. Telemetry is now common enough that few users think about it. But the ones who do can get very upset if they think you are doing them wrong. You want to at least consider getting users' permission to collect their data and allowing them to opt out. How should we think about this?

First, permission may not apply if you are writing enterprise applications, that is, for use by employees in a business. US courts have long held that the computer belongs to the employer, which can look at anything it wants to. Some nasty employers go so far as to use keystroke trackers to find employees who are goofing off instead of madly typing away. It can be trickier in the EU, and other regulations may apply. But in general, the more control the employer has over the computer, the less permission is needed for monitoring users. Check the law so you know at least the minimum standard you have to meet.

If you are not in an enterprise situation, it is a very good idea to provide users with the capability of turning off your telemetry. Few users are paying enough attention to notice, and fewer still would care if they did. But the ones who do care can get upset and make a fuss, which you certainly don't need. Allowing users an easy way to turn it off means that anyone who gets seriously offended by it can have what he wants and will then (you hope) go away and find someone else to annoy.

Most apps provide this option deep in their settings page, as it doesn't (OK, shouldn't) affect the actual operation of the program. Firefox, for example, provides access to it on its Options → Advanced tab, as shown in Figure 5.5.

Once we've made our telemetry configurable, we have to figure out what its default state should be. There aren't all that many choices; there's on, there's off, and there's ask-the-user, with no apparent consensus in the marketplace. Firefox turns it off by default for regular user versions. Google Chrome calls it "Usage Statistics" and turns it on by default. Microsoft programs generally ask permission at installation time, sometimes with the enabling box checked by default and sometimes not.

With mobile apps, the situation is murkier. When you install a mobile app, it provides a screen telling you the features of your device that it needs to access and asking your permission to do so. Figure 5.6 shows the permission request screen for Skype on a Nexus 5 phone. You can see that it wants to use the device's camera and location, among other things.

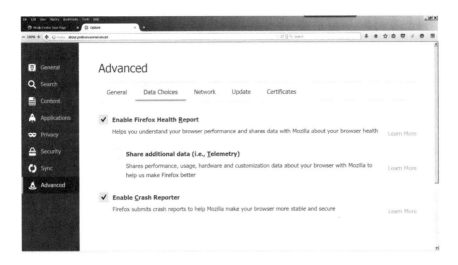

Figure 5.5 Telemetry configuration in Firefox.

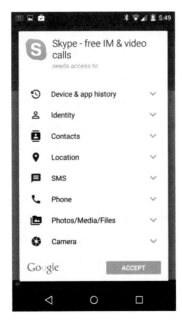

Figure 5.6 Privilege request screen for Skype on Android. There's no mention of telemetry permission.

What you do not see is any permission request for telemetry. How will Skype's developers know if you're holding the phone in landscape or portrait orientation? Or how many times you had to dial the number before you got it right? And so on. Skype for Windows PC contains an advanced dialog box setting, "Help improve Skype . . . by automatically sending us periodic reports . . . ," which is unchecked by default. The mobile version does not have this check box.

In the fine print of Skype's privacy policy, you can see the words "We collect this information in a variety of ways, including . . . the Skype software on your computer or other device." That appears to be the permission for telemetry, which you automatically accept when you use the program.

It goes back to what I said in my book *Why Software Sucks* (Addison-Wesley, 2007), that privacy policies are useless. They all boil down to this: "We do what the heck we want. And if you don't like it, tough. Don't use our app then." It would seem that most users are comfortable with that.

Selecting a Telemetry Provider

Recording, uploading, storing, and displaying your telemetry information is a nontrivial undertaking. Fortunately a number of companies provide frameworks that accomplish all this with very little effort on your part. You should choose one of these commercial providers rather than rolling your own framework. They vary by cost, and by the degree of handholding that you get. Almost all of them have a free level to get you started.

A book of this type can't provide a comprehensive guide to the telemetry marketplace. As with everything else in the software business, it changes too fast. But here are some programs that are worth looking into: PreEmptive Solutions provides a free version of its telemetry package with Visual Studio, alongside its more widely known product Dotfuscator. It's free and convenient and easy to integrate with development tools. In the example application discussed later in this chapter, we use Xamarin Insights, for the same reason. Microsoft is rolling out its new Application Insights on the Azure platform, which looks good. Google Analytics certainly has big company backing. A friend of mine swears by Localytics. Poke around; they're not hard to find.

You also want to coordinate with your software quality assurance department. They are probably using some sort of telemetry package to monitor your app for crashes and hangs (or at least they should be). Telemetry has been used for that purpose for longer than our usage of monitoring UX. I remember Steve Ballmer crowing about its success at TechEd in 2004, years before Microsoft brought out any UX telemetry. You might as well start by looking at whatever framework your QA people currently use to see if it can handle your UX telemetry needs as well. The newer ones tend to do this well; the older ones tend not to.

Selecting a telemetry provider is especially tricky when your programs run on an internal network that isn't connected to the Internet. Some of my financial clients are in this situation, and a few medical clients as well. Just as a basic hygienic precaution, not a byte gets into or out of their network, no way, nohow; period, stop, end of conversation. How can you do telemetry in this case?

The answer is that some telemetry providers will lease or sell you their server software, which you then run on your private network. It costs more, and you have the headache of administration. But it's far better than no telemetry at all when you are in this high-security situation.

What to Track

As with any other type of investigation, the success or failure of your telemetry project will depend on asking the right questions. What sorts of questions should you be asking with your telemetry? You need to think clearly about the insights you want to gain from it.

For starters, stay away from low-level stuff. UX telemetry isn't about tracking the internal flow of your software. It's not for tracking that function A called B called C called D, returning 1, returning 2, returning 3, returning zero. That's for your debugging tools. You certainly shouldn't be doing that on a customer system.

You should be thinking more in terms of highest-level functionality, such as "The user opened a document, then opened a second one, spell-checked the first, printed the second, then closed them both." The buzzwords *key performance indicators* are thrown around a lot. Obviously these will vary from one type of program to another, but here are some general thoughts.

Tracking feature usage is often a major goal of telemetry. When Microsoft Office, the largest application in common usage, first got telemetry, one of the main things Microsoft wanted to know was how often each of Office's hundreds of features actually got used. A source on the Office team told me they were astonished by how few of its features were widely used. Every Office developer thought that the feature she worked on was the one that users couldn't live without. She dedicated her life to it, all day, every day; of course the world would stop turning without it, no? But no, only 1% of users ever opened the equation editor, or the table of authorities, and so on. Who knew?

You might want to track sequences of operations. Consider the Insert key on the Windows keyboard. In Word, when you hit that key, you got switched into overtype mode. I have never seen, or even heard of, anyone doing that because she wanted to. I've only ever seen it as an infuriating accident, but I didn't have data to prove that most users shared my view. To find this answer, you would track the Insert key and the Undo key and see how often the user undid whatever she did in overtype mode. Microsoft eventually got that data, which did indeed prove that I was right, and turned this feature off by default. (You can reenable it on the Advanced settings, if you care enough to go searching for it.)

If your program has a Help system, you definitely want to track the topics that users ask for help on. That will tell you the parts of your user interface that aren't clear to users.

You might want to consider tracking in which dialog boxes the user most often clicks Cancel instead of OK. It might mean that users bring up that box by mistake. Perhaps the menu item leading to it is unclear.

Telemetry Example

To show a good example of telemetry, an example in which readers and students can participate, we'll look at a mobile phone app. Xamarin is a platform that allows you to develop apps for Android, iPhone, and Windows Phone from a single codebase, using C# in Visual Studio. It's a good place from which to demonstrate telemetry as well.

We'll start with Xamarin's BugSweeper sample app, written by the one and only Charles Petzold. (I first learned Windows programming, the 16-bit SDK in C, from his famous book back in the day.) It's conceptually similar to the Minesweeper app you find in Windows, alongside Solitaire. The sample app comes in iPhone, Android, and Windows Phone flavors. Figure 5.7 shows a screenshot from a Nexus 5.

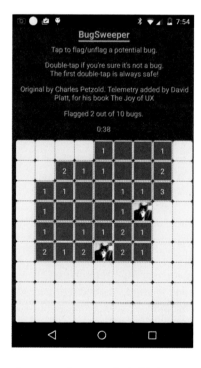

Figure 5.7 BugSweeper sample app running on an Android phone.

The first design decision we need to make is choosing a telemetry provider. Because we are already using the Xamarin mobile framework, it's easiest to use Xamarin's own telemetry provider, called Xamarin Insights. It works well and is simple to use, and it has a free level of usage to entice you and get you started. It is very much aimed at integrating crash recording with UX tracking.

The main competitor for this particular sample was Google Analytics, which has the capability of tracking mobile apps. It is much more flexible and more powerful than Xamarin Insights, but also much more complicated. Amazon currently shows six separate books dedicated to it. The work required to splice it into this project would have been overkill for this small example.

Going to Insights.Xamarin.com brings up a developer tool subscription login. On the Insights main page, XI requires us to "create an app," which is somewhat confusing. If we already have an app, one that works well, would this create a new blank project or something? When we click on that link, we find that by "create an app," XI means to "enable telemetry on an existing Xamarin app." One could argue that *register* would be a clearer verb than *create*. It gives us a unique key, a text string that we will use in our code to differentiate our app from all the other apps that XI tracks. Figure 5.8 shows this screen.

We then download and install the XI packages into our development environment. That doesn't take long. We also have to add code to our app's initialization function to initialize XI. Here it is in Listing 5.2.

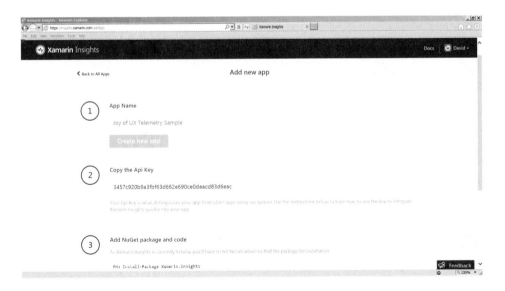

Figure 5.8 Creating an app in Xamarin Insights.

Listing 5.2 Initialization Code for Xamarin Insights

```
public class MainActivity : FormsApplicationActivity
{
        protected override void OnCreate(Bundle bundle)
        {

            // Start Insights

            Insights.Initialize(
              "3457c920b9a3fbf63d662e690cedaacd83d6eac",
              Android.App.Application.Context);
        }
}
```

When the app initializes, it sets up communication with XI to track a number of useful items, such as crashes. The Audience tab of the reports, shown in Figure 5.9, shows some interesting items ("Know Thy User, for He Is Not Thee"). You can see the number of users that you get, the countries they come from, the languages they use. You can see the number of daily sessions. How addictive is your game? You can see operating systems and top devices. This gives you a pretty good pulse on your user base. This is great information to have, especially considering the tiny amount of work and money you had to expend to get it.

Now we want to track key performance indicators, data that is specifically about our game. What should these be? Any game developer knows that a game has to have just the right balance of challenge to be successful. If it's too easy, users quickly get tired of it and walk away.

Figure 5.9 Audience tab in Xamarin Insights.

They do the same if it's too hard. So the first thing we need to know about the game is whether the users are winning it or not.

Xamarin Insights allows you to track your own items. These are called "Events." An event is anything at all in your program that you want to know about and make a call to track. Let's have an event called "GameWon" and another called "GameLost." In our (actually Petzold's) end of the game code, we'll add calls to XI to track these events.

We also want to know how long each game lasted. At the beginning of the game, Petzold starts a timer to display on the screen. At the end of the game we read that timer and track the results. We want to track the elapsed time in seconds, but here's a snag: If a game goes on for a long time—say, the person starts playing it, gets distracted, puts the phone back in a pocket, then doesn't come back to it for a week—that huge value would throw off any sort of scaling in displaying the results. So after we fetch the elapsed time, if the game took longer than ten minutes (600 seconds), we'll truncate it to 600 seconds. If we get a whole lot of these, we'll need to rethink the way we're recording times (and also how users are playing the game).

A game that you lose probably takes a whole lot less time than a game that you win. So we'll record the duration of the game in the same event with which we recorded the win or loss. Listing 5.3 shows our call to XI.

Listing 5.3 Making a Call to XI to Track a Custom Game Event

```
int GameSeconds ;

if (hasWon)
{
        // Track a win, with the elapsed time

        Insights.Track("GameWon", "Time", GameSeconds.ToString());

        DisplayWonAnimation();
}
```

Finally, say we're also curious as to how our customers hold their phones while they're playing. It's probably not a huge deal right now, as the game board is square. But if we ever want to make it rectangular, we'll need to know in what direction to extend it. We go to the correct place in the sample code, fetch the orientation from the Xamarin frameworks, and track it in XI. One could make a case that since Xamarin is a development environment for mobile apps, XI should automatically track this for you, but it currently doesn't. For the wish list, perhaps.

We could think about tracking individual users. Are 20% of our users playing 80% of our games? How does winning percentage improve over time? Tracking individual users is not hard in XI. You assign each user a unique code, a large random number that you generate the first time

Figure 5.10   Xamarin Insights showing events from the sample app.

the app starts up on a device. You never associate it with a person's identity, so it stays anonymous. XI makes it easy to associate your events with a specific user. But that is more work than necessary for this simple example. We'll pass on it for now until we examine the basic data to see what it's telling us.

I published my sample app on the Google Play app store, for free. I then sent an email to everyone in my contacts list and publicized it on every social media app that I use, asking users to download it and run it a while so I could see the results. Figure 5.10 shows a quick look at some of them. The user won 15 games, and the most frequent time was 28 seconds.

I wish that I could download the raw data so I could slice and dice it with my own analytical tools. Xamarin does not provide this capability at the time of this writing, though it is by far the most requested feature and is said to be coming soon.

Suggestions for Telemetry Today

After working with telemetry for some years, I've come to the following conclusions about how we should be using it today:

- Telemetry is a fundamental part of today's standard of care. It is not optional. Without it, you cannot possibly make design decisions as well as you need to. If you do not use telemetry, the developers who do will clean your clock. Fortunately, as we've seen, the impact of adding the telemetry code is minimal.

- Once you acknowledge that you need telemetry, it follows that you need to bake telemetry into your app from the very beginning. Don't fall into the trap of saying, "We'll get the app working right, then we'll start thinking about splicing in the telemetry for version 2." How can you possibly know if version 1 of your app is working right if you don't have the information from telemetry? Starting small is just fine, desirable even. But you need to know how that small piece is working before you can enlarge it.

- Start your data collection small. Telemetry can easily overwhelm you. I've seen this candy store mentality, where developers who are new to telemetry grab at everything in sight. Don't give in to this. Start by collecting small and manageable sets of data, as we did in our example program. This data will suggest what you should look at next.

- Be very careful to understand and comply with the customer's expectation of privacy, whatever that might be. It's a good idea to provide the capability of turning telemetry off. Few users will take you up on it, nowhere near enough to change your statistical validity. Think long and hard before you collect any data that is personally identifiable.

- And finally, you *must* understand that telemetry is *never* the whole story. It is absolutely necessary, but it is nowhere near sufficient. It is a complement to lab testing, not a replacement for it. You also need to coordinate it with user data you get from other channels such as tech support. Each of these communication channels has different sets of advantages and drawbacks, showing you different aspects of the users' total experience but hiding others. Only by looking at them all together can you synthesize the whole picture.

Getting Telemetry Wrong

Here's a classic example of getting telemetry wrong. It reminds me of the Sherlock Holmes story that featured a dog that didn't bark:

Microsoft released Windows 8 in August of 2012. It featured a drastically changed user interface layout intended to support tablet-based devices. As a result, it didn't have the Windows Start menu in its lower left corner, as had every version of Windows for the previous 17 years. Microsoft thought that users wouldn't miss it. Microsoft was wrong.

Microsoft made this decision because its telemetry reported that users rarely used the Start menu. For frequently used programs, users pinned icons on the taskbar. For infrequently used programs, they clicked on the Start button and typed characters into a text box, where the auto-search located them faster than menu selection could. Microsoft therefore thought that users didn't need or want the Start menu anymore.

History records the result. Windows 8 was extremely unpopular with mainstream PC users, flopping even worse than Windows Vista, which is saying something. The lack of a Start menu was one of the main reasons. For users who did adopt Windows 8, a replacement Start menu was by far the most popular add-on app.

Microsoft did not realize that, even though users rarely navigated via the Start menu, they found its mere presence to be reassuring. When users first saw Windows 8, they invariably looked for this orientation point and didn't find it. They felt disoriented, as if Microsoft had pulled the rug out from under them. They didn't say, "Wow, Microsoft, you're every bit as cool as Apple. Thank you for turning my world upside down." They said, "WTF? Where am I?" And they didn't like it one tiny bit.

Microsoft had to restore the Start menu with the release of Windows 10. The fact that Microsoft skipped over Windows 9 in the numbering scheme shows how eager the company is to distance today's product from Windows 8.

How could Microsoft have avoided this misstep? Again, telemetry is necessary, but not sufficient. Microsoft's other channels of user research should have shown them this problem when they tried it on early users. But Windows 8 was a classic example of an echo chamber, where the team heard only their own internal feedback saying how cool they all agreed that they were and ignored anything that didn't fit their own preconceptions.

They forgot that their user wasn't them. And they got what happens whenever any developer forgets that. Don't let that be you.

CHAPTER 6

SECURITY AND PRIVACY

You might wonder why a book on UX has a chapter about security. Isn't security the domain of the geekiest geeks? Mathematical wizards like Alan Turing, considered weird even by programmer standards? Isn't it all about cryptography?

Nothing could be further from the truth. As security guru Bruce Schneier wrote in his classic book *Secrets and Lies* (Wiley, 2000), "If you think technology can solve your security problems, then you don't understand the problems and you don't understand the technology." User interaction and behavior dictate the success or failure of *all* security. Come, hear my words, and understand.

Everything's a Trade-off

The only computer that's completely safe is one that's turned off, unplugged, sealed in concrete, and buried ten feet in the ground. But you can't get much work done on one of those. So any sort of computer usage involves some form of compromise between usability and security. Choosing the right compromises for your application is the difference between success and failure of your project. And avoiding complete boneheaded idiocy doesn't hurt either.

Security has not historically been viewed as the realm of UX. But by understanding who our users are, what they're trying to do, and what benefit they expect from doing it, we can generate some notion of the amount of security-related effort they'll tolerate and channel that effort into the areas that will provide the most safety. That's our job—to understand users and shape the application for their maximum benefit.

Not that we should demand the keys to the security kingdom. The *uber*-geeks won't hand them over, and we don't really want them anyway. And there are levels of it that we have no business touching. But you and I, the advocates for our user population, need to take our place at the table to guide the trade-offs. Because if our application gets the UX wrong, all security is out the window, and our products are, too.

Users Are Human

I recently attended a talk on computer security at which the speaker described a particular bad-guy exploit and asked, "Why does this happen?" A guy in the audience behind me yelled out, "Because users are stupid."

The speaker (whom I greatly respect) let the comment pass. But at the end of the talk, I stood up and announced in my auditorium-filling voice, "To the gentleman who said that users are stupid: Users are human. And they will remain human for the foreseeable future. If you expect them to change into something else, then you're the one that's stupid."

What are humans like? Figure 6.1 shows some ideas. They are innumerate (the mathematical analog of "illiterate"—that's why the gambling industry can exist). They are lazy. They are distractible. They are uncooperative. They are, in a word, *human*.

Years ago, we required human users to adapt to the requirements of their software, to become "computer literate" in the idiom of the day. By now you've absorbed the message of this book: that day has long since passed, and it is now our job to adapt our software to our users.

In those early days, we didn't have the Internet continuously connecting every intelligent device on the planet to every other intelligent device on the planet. If typing keyboard commands into a *Star Trek* game, as we had to do then, was more difficult than clicking a mouse as we do now, at least we didn't have to worry about bad guys stealing the passwords to our bank

(a)   (b)

(c)   (d)

Figure 6.1   Humans are (a) innumerate, (b) lazy, (c) distractible, and (d) uncooperative—in a word: human. (Photo by Antoine Taveneaux/Photos © iStock.com/Spauln tap10 and Michael Krinke)

accounts while we played. We didn't have our retail purchases online, or our financial affairs, or our medical data. We didn't have security threats evolving from script kiddies to the Russian mafia to foreign sovereign nations. The world was simpler and safer then.

While threats to our security keep escalating, users keep demanding apps that are easier to use. For example, many banks would like to demand two-factor authentication, with a password and a phone message, but users resist this extra effort even when it's done for their safety. Usability guys like us are caught in a nutcracker. But hey, if it was easy, anyone could do it.

What Users *Really* Care About

If you ask users if security is important to them, they will always answer yes. Very important? Yes, of course, very, very important. But at the same time, security is never a user's prime goal. When the user's wife calls down to the basement, "Bob, what are you doing now?" does the guy

Figure 6.2   Humans are two-faced. This statue is 2,000 years old. This is not a new problem. (Photo by Loudon Dodd)

ever yell back, "I'm being secure!"? No. He's balancing his checkbook or playing Zork or whatever. Any distraction from that, for security or anything else, is unwelcome.

Users say they want security but are unwilling to divert any effort to it. As Alma Whitten and J. D. Tygar wrote in the book *Security and Usability* (ed. Cranor and Garfinkel, O'Reilly, 2005), "[Users] do not generally sit down at their computers wanting to manage their security; rather, they want to send email, browse web pages, or download software, and they want security in place to protect them while they do those things. It is easy for [users] to put off learning about security, or to optimistically assume that their security is working, while they focus on their primary goals."

Like defending our country, users feel it's very, very important, but they want someone else to do it. In addition to all the qualities mentioned before, humans are two-faced. They'll say one thing and do exactly the opposite and see nothing contradictory about their actions. The statue in Figure 6.2 is 2,000 years old. This is not a new problem.

As Jesper Johansson, today a Senior Principal Security Engineer at Amazon, has said to me many times, "Given a choice between dancing pigs and security, users will pick dancing pigs every time." This is the bargain that we accept when we go into this end of the business.

The Hassle Budget

Because users are human, they view any effort required for security as a distraction, an unwelcome intrusion, a tax. Therefore, they will tolerate only a limited amount of it. I have coined the term *hassle budget* to describe this amount of effort. If your application exceeds your users' hassle budget, they will either figure out a workaround or toss your app.

Consider the following example. You probably have a lock on the front door of your house. The lock requires a certain amount of effort to install initially, then some amount of effort to carry a key and use it every time you enter your house. You accept this overhead because you consider it small compared to its benefit: keeping random strangers out of your home. This effort is within your hassle budget.

Suppose now that your landlord installed a combination lock on the door of your bathroom inside the house, with spring hinges to automatically close and latch the door. You would probably consider the effort to work this lock every time you need to go to be much larger than the benefit the lock provides. It now exceeds your hassle budget.

How long would you tolerate this? Once, certainly, to get the door open initially. Perhaps twice. No way, nohow, would you do it a third time. Uninstalling it isn't an option because the landlord holds the power and decrees that you shall have the lock. So you would perform some sort of workaround—tape down the latch, prop the door open with a chair, or say, "To hell with this," and go piss in the kitchen sink.

Because the landlord's imposed security requirements exceed your hassle budget, the bathroom actually becomes less secure than it was before. The usual bathroom privacy lock, easily defeated with a screwdriver, provided a polite reminder: "Bathroom in use. Please follow the rules." With the tape or the chair workaround, you've lost even that rudimentary level. And with the kitchen sink workaround, you've lost that customer.

And take this thought one step further. The landlord thinks that because he's installed the combination lock, the bathroom's security is higher than before. But instead it is actually lower, because the more stringent requirement exceeded the tenant's hassle budget and triggered the workaround. The landlord now has the *worst possible* sense of security: a false one.

That's exactly what users do with computer security requirements. If you exceed their hassle budget, they'll either figure out a workaround or say to hell with it and get rid of your app. Figure 6.3 shows one sort of workaround. And you then have either a system that's as secure as the workaround, or no customers. Like an ancient Greek tragedy, the more security engineers struggle against insecure users, the less secure they all become.

Hassle budgets are highly subjective. They vary by user, by the benefit the users perceive they will gain from your app, and by the ease of getting that same benefit somewhere else. Aunt Millie's hassle budget is very low for the genealogy program, slightly higher for seeing pictures of her grandchildren's high school graduation, but never all that large for anything. She won't spend time struggling with a computer, for security or any other reason. What do you think she'll do if her family photo Web site demands that she change her password every three months and insists on a strong password that contains upper- and lowercase letters, a number, and a symbol? She'll say, "Heck with it," and go off to knit or play bridge or watch Turner Classic Movies on cable. She knows that her grandson will be delighted to show off those pictures on

Figure 6.3   Users *will* employ a workaround if their hassle budget has been exceeded. (Photo by Jake Ludington)

his new iPhone the next time he comes to visit. On the other hand, 15-year-old techno-nerd Elmer (whiz-bang programmer, terrible at sports, bedeviled by acne, shunned by girls) will do almost anything to obtain undocumented cheat codes to his favorite games. His hassle budget in this case is much higher. (By the way, do you see the power of personas for illustrating this example?)

Respect Your Users' Hassle Budget

You may think that the hassle budget and its workarounds are wrong and bad and stupid. You may think that further education will cause users to accede to your demands for greater security effort. You'd be wrong. I've seen user education touted as the solution to security concerns for at least 20 years. If it were going to work, it would have by now. Why hasn't it, and what should we do instead?

Cormac Herley, a scientist at Microsoft Research, has published some good papers on the interaction of security with users. I especially admire a brilliant one of his entitled "So Long, and No Thanks for the Externalities: The Rational Rejection of Security Advice by Users." I strongly urge you to find this paper and read it completely.

Herley has a new take on users' hassle budgets: they are not wrong or stupid. He argues that the professionals who prescribe security advice to users rarely weigh the cost of following that advice against the harm that advice would prevent if users indeed followed it. He says that "users' rejection of the security advice they receive is entirely rational from an economic perspective. The advice offers to shield them from the direct costs of attacks, but burdens them with far greater indirect costs in the form of effort."

Consider an attack that hits one user out of 100 every year, and it takes the targeted user ten hours to clean up after it. The total cost of this exploit is thus 36,000 seconds per year per 100 users, or 360 seconds per user per year. If the user action required to prevent this exploit consumes more than about one second per day, the treatment is, overall, worse than the disease. An ounce of cure is not worth five pounds of prevention.

Herley continues (my emphasis added):

> There are about 180 million online adults in the US. At twice the US minimum wage one hour of user time is then worth $7.25 * 2 * 180 million = $2.6 billion. . . . This places things in an entirely new light. We suggest that the main reason security advice is ignored is that it makes an enormous miscalculation: it treats as free a resource that is actually worth $2.6 billion an hour. It's not uncommon to regard users as lazy or reluctant. A better understanding of the situation might ensue if *we viewed the user as a professional who bills at $2.6 billion per hour,* and whose time is far too valuable to be wasted on unnecessary detail.

I just saw an article on the Web entitled "Thirty-Seven Ways to Prevent Identity Theft." If I have to do 37 different things to keep my identity safe, forget it. The bad guys can have the damn thing.

The key, as I've said throughout this book, is to understand the user. It is to figure out what the user *really* wants and needs, to weigh the costs of prevention versus cleanup, and ruthlessly trim, automate, and optimize the efforts we require of our users.

A Widespread, Real-Life, Hassle Budget Workaround

Here's an example of the users' hassle budget and the security mafia's cluelessness as to how to manage it.

Highly paid security gurus pontificate that your password should be random so as to be unguessable (not your wife's name, or children's, or dog's, etc.). OK, that makes sense; I've cracked a few by guessing the obvious choices. That's why I always use a random generator when I need to choose a new password. (See Figure 6.4 for the logical conclusion of this idea.) Then they'll say that you shouldn't write it down. Again, I can see the logic of this. That's one of the ways that Richard Feynman cracked classified safes on the atomic bomb project during the Second World War and left goofy notes, which drove the security people batty. (See his autobiography, *Surely You're Joking, Mr. Feynman,* for the other two ways.) Then they'll tell you to use a different password for every account you have. Like the other two, it makes sense on its own. Then, finally, they'll tell you to change them all periodically.

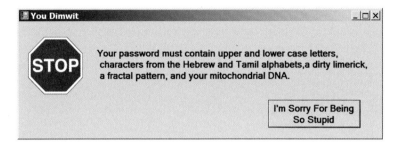

Figure 6.4   Logical conclusion of password advice.

Human beings cannot do all four of these things together. Our brains aren't built that way; that's why we invented computers. You can get any two of these things at once, if you're lucky. Telling users to do all of them while knowing, *knowing* that they can't, instead of figuring out how to be as secure as you can with what users actually can (and sometimes even will) do, constitutes malpractice.

Which of these items offers the least bang for the buck? Which spends the users' hassle budget least wisely? Probably the last one: changing your passwords every so often. Here's why:

In mathematical theory, periodic changes make a small amount of sense. Changing a password provides some protection against a bad guy's brute-force attack on a stolen password file. It does not protect at all against a password stolen by a keystroke logger, or by shoulder surfing, or by phishing. Nor does it solve the problem of a user handing over credentials to a bad guy in return for money or sex or revenge. Are you sure there's no one like that in your network?

If an even-halfway-competent bad guy steals a password, he knows that it will probably have a very short lifetime, like a stolen credit card number. He will therefore use it immediately, trying to steal the maximum amount before the exploit gets noticed and the account locked. The three-month or six-month password reset interval won't help us here, because the bad guy will almost certainly not encounter it before other security mechanisms kick in.

So this security fix, *if it works*, only solves the problem of someone stealing a password, and then remaining undetected while observing on the network, like (say) Yahoo spying on (say) Microsoft's internal telephone directory to woo key employees away. (Of course, if Yahoo really wanted Microsoft employees, a full-page ad in the *Seattle Times* offering large cash bonuses would probably work better.)

A case might still exist for changing passwords to prevent this last exploit, if such changes did indeed work. But periodic password changes backfire on administrators because their user population is human—in this case, the uncooperative and lazy part of being human. Think about the trodden path in Figure 6.1d, which is called a "desire line." Were the walkers being asked for too much, to deviate from their path by a few feet to stay on the pavement and keep the grass nice? The askers didn't think so, but the walkers, with their behavior, said yes. It exceeded their hassle budget. They wouldn't cooperate.

And neither will users when they are required to change their passwords. I have never, and I mean not once ever in my entire life, seen or even heard of users doing anything other than changing the last character of their passwords, almost always a number in ascending sequence, so they can remember it from one mandated change to the next. They might start with a random password (if they're forced to), such as w5NCzr#@h. But when they have to change it, they'll add a suffix to make w5NCzr#@h1. The next one will be w5NCzr#@h2 and so on. The real irony here is that the more random you make the rest of the password, the more the repetitive pattern sticks out. Do you think even a script-kiddie-level bad guy won't figure it out? My daughter did, at age ten. Because users feel that this requirement exceeds their hassle budget, they perform a minimum-effort workaround that gets the security nazis off their back.

Microsoft has 128,000 employees. Changing passwords quarterly, figuring ten minutes per change, costs Microsoft over 85,000 employee hours per year, roughly the equivalent of 42 full-time employees. That doesn't count the time consumed by resets of forgotten passwords, increased tech support line costs, or the opportunity cost of locked-out employees. Is Microsoft getting value for its money? I think not.

The only way to solve this password-changing problem would be to assign each user a new random password every quarter. Of course, users can't (won't) remember those, so they will (as always) perform a workaround by writing them down. The new passwords would then be as secure as the sticky notes that they're written on. Again: Greek tragedy.

So why do companies force users to change their passwords? When I ask the people in charge of such matters, I get two different answers. The first is that many security administrators actually believe that it works. This is scary, because it would mean that the people who are in charge of watching our backs are incompetent. I hope it really means that they aren't willing to admit that they know it doesn't, or at least not admit it to me. Sometimes they'll say, "We have a user education program that takes care of that." They may well have a user education program, but I'd bet my house it doesn't take care of that.

The second, smaller, group admits that, no, they probably don't derive any benefit from periodic password changes, certainly nothing proportionate to the user time it consumes. But they say that, since it shows up on some best practice lists, they don't have the authority to change it. It's security theater, a placebo to show the masses, or their technologically illiterate bosses, that *something is being done*. They sometimes quote the serenity prayer ("God grant me the serenity to accept the things I cannot change, the courage to change the things I can, and the wisdom to know the difference"). And they say that they want to save their political capital for things that really do matter.

And finally, the security administrators are not paying the bill for the user time that these policies waste. In fact, another excellent paper by Cormac Herley ("Where Do Security Policies

Come From?," coauthored with Dinei Florêncio) finds the most stringent policies not where the need is the greatest, measured by either assets guarded or number of attacks. Rather, they find that the strongest security policies are at .edu and .gov domains, which are "better insulated from the consequences of imposing poor usability decisions on their users." To those decisions and their consequences we now turn our attention.

Case Study: Amazon.com

Amazon is one of the most successful companies ever. It therefore stands to reason that the trade-offs Amazon makes between security and usability are effective ones for their user population. They are tight enough to hold losses to an acceptable level and to keep users comfortable with shopping there. And they are lenient enough that they don't obstruct users from giving Amazon their money—lots and lots of their money. Let's examine these trade-offs.

Originally founded to sell paper books (remember them?), and then CDs (them too?), Amazon now sells anything and everything, physical or digital. Its Kindle reader has redefined what it means to read a book or to write one. Their patented 1-Click order system is so effective at facilitating impulse purchases that I had to turn the damn thing off because I was buying too much stuff.

When you first bring up Amazon's Web page, it is completely generic (Figure 6.5). It shows what other people are buying, but nothing tailored for you. You can search for products and add them to the cart.

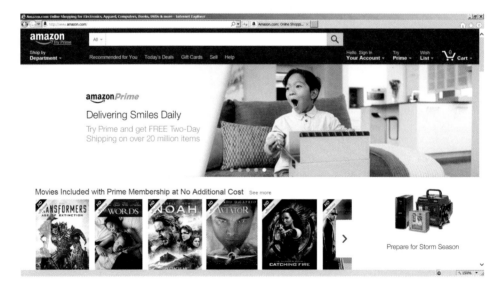

Figure 6.5 Generic Amazon home page shown to users who are not yet authenticated.

If you want to buy something or check your orders, you have to log in. Note that Amazon at this point (Figure 6.6) does not offer the check box that says "Keep me signed in."

Now that it knows who you are, Amazon's home page shows items that Amazon thinks you are likely to want, based on previous purchases (Figure 6.7). You can check out, view your wish list, view or modify previous orders, and so on, as a logged-in user would expect. So far, so standard.

Now, close your browser, reopen it, and go back to Amazon. It still (or again) presents your personalized view as shown in Figure 6.7. It does this by default, even though you didn't ask

Figure 6.6   Generic Amazon login screen. Note the absence of a "Keep me signed in" check box.

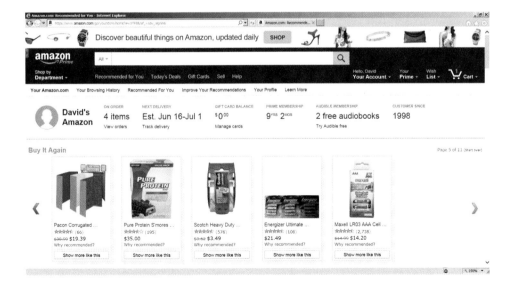

Figure 6.7   Amazon home page shown after the user first logs in.

Amazon to keep you logged in, and even though Amazon didn't offer you the option to do that. What's going on here?

Like most businesses, Amazon makes most of its money from repeat purchasers, and the UX is optimized for this. Amazon figures that since it's identified you once, and no one else has logged in to Amazon on this computer since, the user is most likely you coming back again, and that both Amazon and you would be happier to pick up where you left off last time.

You aren't fully logged in at this point. You are in a sort of twilight, semi-authenticated state. "We think you are probably [this person], but we are not sure. Therefore, we will go so far with you and no farther," Amazon thinks. You can view your recommendations from this screen, Amazon's primary mechanism for encouraging you to buy more stuff. You can see or modify your wish list. You can order items via 1-Click, if you've set that up previously. Because you have already successfully shipped items to your 1-Click address, Amazon figures that it's OK to do that again without further authentication.

If you want to use the standard checkout or view your orders, you need to log in again. Amazon will automatically take you to the login page when you click on any link that requires authentication. Note that when you log in from this intermediate state, the login screen prefills your email address and also contains a check box that allows you to stay logged in (Figure 6.8). If you check this box, Amazon will keep you logged in for two weeks. You can check your orders or buy things from your cart without further authentication. But if you want to change your account settings, such as adding addresses, you have to log in again at that time. And if you want to ship something to an address that you have not previously used, you need to enter your credit card number again at that time.

Figure 6.8   Amazon login screen on a PC where Amazon thinks it knows the user. Note the prefilled email address field, and the presence of a "Keep me signed in" check box.

Table 6.1   Amazon User Privileges Based on Most Recent Authentication

Privilege	Most Recent Authentication
View recommendations, use wish list, buy with 1-Click	Anytime (as long as you haven't explicitly signed out)
Buy via shopping cart, view or change orders	Current session, or within two weeks if you selected "Keep me signed in" at last authentication
Change account settings	Current session only

You see that Amazon provides a hierarchy of escalating privileges, based on how recently you have authenticated. These levels are shown in Table 6.1.

Obviously, you might be viewing Amazon on someone else's computer. It might be someone you trust, say, a family member. Or it might be in an untrusted environment, such as the public library. Amazon provides you the capability to explicitly log out and wipe your history. But that takes work to find and to use. The Sign Out menu option is buried at the bottom of the Your Account dropdown (Figure 6.9). Even the label suggests that it's not for ordinary usage—"Not David? Sign Out." How about "Paranoid David in Public Library? Sign Out." I would be curious as to what Amazon's telemetry says is the percentage of users who ever do this.

Amazon has calculated that its biggest profits come from ongoing relationships, from being the users' default option when they need to buy something. Just finished the last of the dental floss? No problemo, order more from your bedside Kindle. "People who bought Tom's of Maine

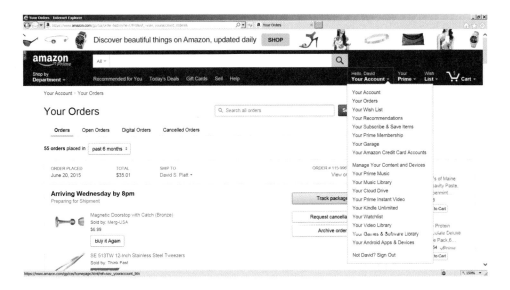

Figure 6.9   Sign Out menu item on the Amazon home page.

brand floss also bought Tom's toothpaste." Want some? Sure, as long as I'm here, why not? We're probably getting low.

That's why Amazon sets the default option to remember the user's identity from one browser session to another: Amazon makes more money that way. Can it backfire? Of course. Suppose you order something from a public library computer and forget to log out from Amazon. The next library patron can see what you were looking at, or what you've recently ordered. It's not all that much work to connect this knowledge to you personally, especially if you live in a small town as I do. A library patron with a nasty sense of humor could order an embarrassing item sent to you via 1-Click.

But Amazon calculates: *Our* users probably won't order from a public PC anywhere near as much as from a home PC. Not never, but a whole lot less. And if they do order from a public PC, they'll probably be paranoid enough to log out after their session. And if they're not, public PCs often restart their desktop sessions after each patron. And if not, maybe the next person won't do anything bad. She could wipe out your wish list or add bad things to it, not a whole lot of harm done, but we bet she won't. And if she does order something, we've limited her to your 1-Click addresses. You'll probably see the order and cancel it. And if not, we'll offer you free return shipping and maybe a $20 credit and you'll probably sing our praises.

Amazon calculates that fixing the errors that do occur with this level of trade-off is more profitable than preventing the possibility by dumping your browser session. Its ubiquitous connection to your life makes the company more money, a *lot* more money, than the bad guys steal from it. It's that ounce of cure again.

Amazon does not insist on strong passwords, nor does it ever make you change a password. As I explained, the latter provides very little additional security. Unlike corporate or government or educational establishments, Amazon *does*, or would, bear the financial burden of bad usability. If a customer comes to Amazon and is told to change her password, she could easily get angry and buy that thing somewhere else on the Web. Amazon usually has good prices, but they're not always the very best anymore. Rather, Amazon offers a trusted name, excellent customer service, and absolutely killer ease of use.

Another reason that Amazon gets away with relatively weak passwords is because passwords are not the only line of defense against bad guys. Amazon ships goods to specific addresses. Once it's successfully shipped to your address, it knows that address is good. A random bad guy somehow ordering something on your account would want it shipped to his own address. But if you want Amazon to ship to a new address, you have to enter the credit card number again. And if the bad guy has stolen your wallet and credit cards, you have more problems than just Amazon.

Amazon also has more security going on behind the scenes. Amazon is constantly checking usage patterns—does this purchase fit your pattern? And the credit card companies backstop

Amazon. Expensive, highly resalable items will be shipped only to the billing address of the credit card. I had a client who tried to send me a computer for a project he wanted me to work on, and Amazon wouldn't ship it directly to me for that reason. Once in a while I get a call from Amazon, or my credit card company: "Did you really order [whatever]?" Almost always, I have. "Great! Thank you for using [whatever]." And if not, they've found the fraud before I ever would and can stop it right away. This is good defense in depth.

I am not saying that Amazon has the optimum balance between security and usability for all apps at all times. It's probably too lenient for your bank, which logs you out automatically after ten or so minutes of inaction. It's probably too stringent for your magazine subscription, which never logs you out no matter what. What you need to learn from this analysis is threefold: first, Amazon has very carefully and thoughtfully adjusted its level of security to balance safety with ease of use; second, Amazon has done that through constantly, repeatedly putting itself in the shoes (Amazon now owns Zappos) of its users; and third, Amazon is making a boatload of money because it is getting the trade-off right. So, too, do you need to carefully adjust your level of security, by putting yourself in your users' shoes.

Securing *Our* Applications

Now that we've seen what users want from their products (complete security, complete usability) and what they're willing to do to get it (as little as possible, down to and including nothing at all), what the heck do we do?

Understand *Our* Users' Hassle Budget

As with most things in UX, there are very few things in security that are absolutely good or absolutely bad under all circumstances. The level of security that is reasonable and appropriate, and that users are willing to tolerate, for the mutual fund company that holds your million-dollar retirement portfolio is way overkill for Candy Crush. Figure out the user's hassle budget at the beginning, and work with it. Who is the user? Get out your persona. What problem is Aunt Millie or Reverend Foster trying to solve, and what would they consider to be the characteristics of a good solution? Get out your stories. Where else could they get the same thing done today, if they don't use your products? Try asking the question "What type of hoops are they willing to jump through to get it?" Phrasing it in this deliberately provocative way will concentrate your mind on minimizing the amount of hassle your apps require from your users.

When you've figured out that hassle budget, then try to figure out what sort of workarounds your users will do if they perceive that your security requirements exceed their hassle budget. In a consumer-type situation, they will often simply walk away from your app, and then you've spent all your money building an expensive paperweight. Users of enterprise systems, who often do not have a choice of which software to use, tend to be more ingenious with workarounds. For example, I've seen situations where users are automatically logged off the network when their PCs have been quiescent for some amount of time. Technical users often resent this, especially if the interval is short, and will write or download applications that stimulate their PC frequently enough to defeat the automatic logout. What workarounds will your users do? Try to make sure that they aren't ones that will kill your app. And if they are, go back and rethink the security situation. Remember the bathroom lock example.

Start with Good Defaults

Again, the default settings of an app are absolutely critical. And nowhere are the default settings more important than in the realm of security.

Few users ever change their default settings. Many don't even know that they can, and others don't know where to start. The rest consider it more trouble than it's worth, or fear damaging a working installation. UI guru Alan Cooper considers changing default settings to be the defining characteristic of an advanced user. Thinking of all the applications I use regularly, there isn't one on which I'd consider myself an advanced user in this sense.

Consider Microsoft Outlook. Like most users, I get a lot of junk mail, usually spam or phishing. Back in the 1990s, I remember right-clicking on an email in my in box, seeing the "Junk" entry on the context menu, and saying, "Ah! Outlook knows about junk mail. Good, I'll use it and try to get rid of some of this garbage." But when I selected that option, Outlook brought up a configuration wizard, asking me questions that I had no idea how to answer. Outlook's junk mail filtering didn't do anything at all right out of the box. It insisted that I think. As any human (lazy, forgetful, uncooperative, etc.) user would, I said to hell with it, closed the wizard, and never touched it again.

The current version of Outlook, however, installs with decent defaults. When a message comes in that is obviously junk (most users don't know how Outlook figures it and don't really care, as long as Outlook gets it right most of the time), it automatically goes to the junk mail folder (Figure 6.10). It's almost always right, and we can easily see and correct when it isn't.

You can configure this behavior if you want to. But this dialog box is difficult to find. You have to right-click on an email message to get the context menu, then open the Junk submenu, then select Junk E-mail Options . . . at the bottom of that one. Telemetry would provide an exact number, but not very many users will ever see this box, let alone change anything in it.

Figure 6.11 shows these default settings. The filter level is Low, catching only the most obvious junk. Messages that are thought to be phishing have their links disabled. If there's a suspicious domain in the email address, you get a warning.

These settings aren't perfect. Any set of defaults will always be a compromise. Not all of these complex setting capabilities are useful (you can, for example, block any messages coming from

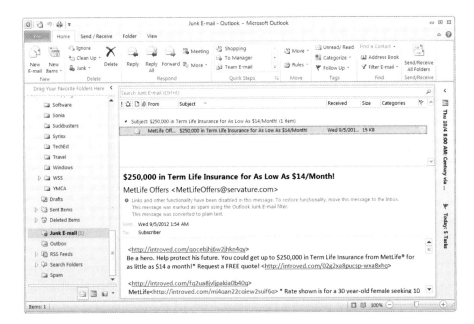

Figure 6.10   Microsoft Outlook default junk mail settings automatically send this spam to the Junk E-mail folder.

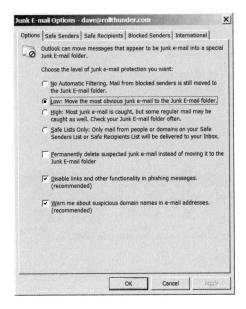

Figure 6.11   Configuration dialog for Outlook's junk mail filter.

Andorra should you wish to), but that's MS and its Office's feature bloat. The company has done a decent job of putting default settings to work. And you need to do that as well.

Decide, Don't Ask

"Dave, come here! My computer is acting weird again!" I hate when my wife calls me from the other end of the house like that. I just know something bad has come up. Something beyond the capability of my daughters—now 13 and 15—and if a teenager can't fix it, you know that it's serious.

She was reacting to a dialog box displayed by Norton Internet Security. Shown in Figure 6.12, the dialog box read, in part: "carboniteservice.exe is attempting to access the Internet. This program has been modified since it was last used." It then went on to ask if the program should be allowed to access the Internet.

What kind of silliness is this? If all the brainpower at Norton can't figure out whether this application should be allowed to access the Internet, how the hell is my wife ever going to?

For that matter, how would you or I, computer professionals that we claim to be, go about figuring it out? We know that the name of the process means nothing at all. Even if we stipulate that Norton is correctly indicating the Carbonite process that we installed, how do we know that Carbonite has been properly updated rather than hijacked by a bad guy, a common attack mode?

We don't, we can't, and we shouldn't be asked to. That's why we buy Norton, to access the top brains in the computer security business. Accepting money for a product called "Internet Security" means knowing how to handle these situations. If the risk is low, Norton shouldn't be bugging me. And if it's not low, Norton shouldn't be saying it is.

What does Norton think it's doing? I spoke at a conference some time ago, next door to an unrelated computer security conference. When I slid over during a break to scarf their free beer

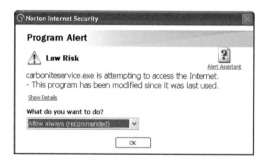

Figure 6.12 Dialog box shown by Norton Internet Security.

(we only had juice), I saw a guy wearing a Norton badge and jumped on him about this dialog box. He said it makes perfect sense to Norton: "We're getting the user's informed consent."

Sorry, that doesn't cut it. Informed consent is consent given when you understand the facts, implications, and future consequences of an action. Ordinary users can't do this, and neither can computer professionals who are not security specialists. Informed consent is impossible in this type of situation.

I opened myself another beer and handed one to the Norton guy, as his meeting was paying for them. He wasn't giving up. "It's like the doctor who tells you the risks and lets you decide," he said.

No, it isn't. Norton throwing this box in a user's face is like an airline asking a passenger if he thinks the weather is safe for flying. The passenger is not competent to make such a judgment. That decision requires professional-grade technical knowledge and rests entirely on trained and licensed professionals who hold responsibility for transporting passengers safely. That model works well for air travel, and we should be working the same way.

The main reason we're seeing this box is likely lawyers. Norton's lawyers told the developers, in effect, "If you're not sure, then just ask the user, and you're off the hook. Then if it breaks, it's the user's own fault." I disagree. It's our job to get it right.

For another example, consider the dialog box in Figure 6.13. It indicates that there is some sort of problem with the security certificate of the target server.

What the heck is going on here? Do you seriously think that Aunt Millie is going to read this box, understand what it means, and make an informed decision about whether to proceed or not? Maybe her sewing circle Web site has been hacked, maybe it hasn't, but this box doesn't help. Not at all.

Figure 6.13 Useless certificate error dialog box.

That's especially true because many legitimate Web sites give you software installation directions telling you to ignore this box. In researching this book, my first page of Google search results showed such instructions coming from UNC Chapel Hill, the government of Oklahoma, and the Consulate General of India, among many others.

Not only does this box not help anything, but it decreases the respect and attention paid to any and all security communications. The "boy crying wolf problem" has been around since at least the time of Aesop (620 BCE), and it probably wasn't new then. It shouldn't surprise anyone when the same actions produce the same results today.

It's especially bad as you will almost never see this message coming from a bad guy's site. As Herley writes, "Attackers wisely calculate that it is far better to go without a certificate than risk the warning. In fact, as far as we can determine, there is no evidence of a single user being saved from harm by a certificate error, anywhere, ever."

Figure 6.14 shows a better example. The page contained some content, probably ads, from servers that had certificate errors. Rather than asking the user, IE simply doesn't display them. It communicates that fact with a bottom bar, far better than a modal dialog box. IE made the decision to err on the side of safety and didn't ask for permission. Someone who depended on the blocked content could probe and try to figure it out, but it doesn't bother most users most of the time. It's a whole lot better than throwing a modal dialog box in the face of someone who cannot possibly know the right answer.

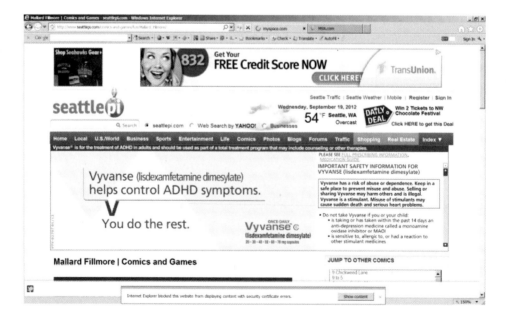

Figure 6.14 Internet Explorer deciding, not asking.

We developers are the experts, and users depend on us. We cannot abdicate our responsibility by asking for guidance from someone who cannot possibly know. Informed consent in computing is a myth, and companies that claim it as an excuse for their malpractice are weasels. Decide, don't ask. If you can't decide, decide anyway. Because your users sure as heck can't decide.

Use Your Persona and Story Skills to Communicate

The geeks who run the security department probably have the least contact with their users of the entire development team. By using your persona and story skills, you can make the users and their hassle budget real to your security developers, so they can truly make informed judgments.

Because we are responsible for the users, it is our job to communicate their needs and concerns to the rest of the design team. This is another reason why the persona and story work needs to be done early, because it will dictate what the security design decisions are, before they are implemented.

Suppose the genealogy program was a Web site, and suppose we were discussing the login requirements. You could say, "Look, here's our user. Her name is Aunt Millie. She's 68 years old, doesn't see too well anymore. Her grandkids are going to set this up for her, but she's the one who's going to be using it day to day. Do we have to make her enter a password every day? Couldn't we let her stay logged in, once we set it up? I don't think we have to worry too much about the cleaning lady turning it on and destroying her family tree."

Try using a story to communicate with the developers, and don't be afraid to play on their heartstrings: "Poor Aunt Millie! She visited the nursing home today, and her mother didn't even recognize her. She drove home in tears. She so desperately fears winding up like that, and she really wants to get these stories out of her brain before that happens to her. She turns on her PC, clicks the desktop icon that her grandson set up for her, and wants our site to load. Damn! The silly computer wants a password. What happened to the password? She looks around, but the sticky note fell off her monitor and she can't find it. Can't we let her stay logged in, like the AARP Web site does?" And so on. Be shameless. I am.

Strengthen Your Stories with Data

One of the main problems with any security decision, as with any other UX decision, is knowing what users actually do, as opposed to what they'll admit to doing or can remember doing. Today we have telemetry to tell us these kinds of things. Since we, as UX, are in charge of much of this telemetry, we can obtain hard data on which to base our hard decisions.

Microsoft SQL Server, for example, used to ship with a built-in administrator account named "sa," with a password that was blank. I made use of this in an earlier book for geeks, to make sample programs that would run right out of the box with no user setup. It sure was convenient. But that's not what passwords are supposed to be for.

SQL Server came with a written checklist of installation instructions, which included changing that password. It was supposed to be installed by a qualified professional, but, being human (lazy, distractible, uncooperative), many of them skipped this step. Bad guys later used this lapse to attack SQL Server over the Internet, causing much *sturm und drang*.

Had we had telemetry then, we would have the data to say, "You know what? Only 65% of SQL administrators actually change their administrator account password from blank. We really ought to think about requiring them to enter one as we run the installer program. We do that for Windows NT. That should be well within the hassle budget of a professional administrator, no? And if they write it down on a sticky note next to their server box, that's still safer than an Internet attack."

You will also have the data to say, "HIPAA [Health Insurance Portability and Accountability Act] regulations require automatic logoff after a system has been inactive for 'a preset amount of time.' When we set it to ten minutes, we find that our nurses have to log on an average of 22 times per day, taking about 30 seconds each. Can we try something else? Maybe a longer timeout interval? How about a fingerprint reader? My bank does that for its tellers, and my pharmacy uses them too. Or maybe an RFID reader that senses the badges we already wear to get into the building? That automatic facial recognition getting built into Windows 10 looks cool. Do you suppose it really works? What happens when a guy shaves off his beard?" And so on.

If you have good usability testing videos, they can also make a big difference in communicating users' feelings. Using the techniques from Chapter 4, you can try various options on the users and record their reactions. Sometimes the videos can speak volumes. It's one thing to say, "Our users got mad and stormed out." It's another thing to actually show the video of them cursing the facilitator up one side, down the other, and throwing the free donuts on the floor.

Cooperate with Other Security Layers

Security is a multilayered heuristic process. Neither user-based security, nor any other layer, can work in the absence of others. The other layers are part of the process and will (at least sometimes) backstop you when your layer fails or gets bypassed.

I once bought a MetroCard (a stored-value fare card) in the New York City subway, paying for it with my credit card. Later that day I decided I needed another MetroCard and tried to buy one. The ticket vending machine accepted my business credit card the first time but rejected it the second time. I called the credit card company, rather annoyed, to see why my good credit wasn't being accepted. The customer service lady told me that that's their loss prevention algorithm. When a card gets stolen, bad guys quickly try to use it before it gets reported and stopped, so they buy things that are easy to resell. MetroCards are about the easiest thing to resell in all of NYC. Everyone in the city needs them, and it's easy to read the remaining value on them. They sell readily for about 50 cents cash on the dollar. So the credit card company will decline a second MetroCard purchase on the same day, figuring it's probably a bad guy. If I wanted, she'd authorize one more, or I could just wait until tomorrow.

This is the sort of thing with which you are cooperating. You are not standing alone. Don't try to solve it all in the user layer, because you can't.

Read a Good Book

You should read the book *Beyond Fear: Thinking Sensibly about Security in an Uncertain World*, by Bruce Schneier (Copernicus, 2006). He is one of the world's top authorities on computer security, and he fully understands the human element; see the quote that opens this chapter. He definitely groks the concept that security measures have a cost as well as (you hope) a benefit. It's fascinating and he writes very well. You need to read it for your own education.

Bury the Hatchet

Security and usability guys often see themselves as adversaries. Scott Adams's famous comic strip fans these flames with a character named Mordac the Preventer. Mordac values security far more than usability, believing that in a perfect world, no user could ever make use of anything. While Dilbert struggles with password requirements, Mordac taunts him with lines from *Deliverance* that I'm stunned he ever got into a family newspaper.

Have you ever tried sitting down with security people and just chatting? Not even necessarily about imminent business, just "Hey, how are you? Don't the Red Sox stink this year?" It's surprising how often no one ever has. They might be a little suspicious at first, but if you don't immediately try telling them how to run their practices, they might open up to you. Invest in a box of donuts once in a while. Pick a specific example from *Beyond Fear* and ask them what they think. Eat lunch with them if you can, maybe offer to start a security-usability discussion group. They'd probably like a little love, and they might settle for just a little less hatred.

The Last Word on Security

I'll give the last word to Cormac Herley, from another excellent paper entitled "More Is Not the Answer" (my emphasis added again):

> It is easy to fall into the trap of thinking that if we find the right words or slogan we can convince people to spend more time on security. Or that usable security offers a bag of tricks to cajole users into increasing effort. We argue that this view is profoundly in error. It presupposes that users are wrong about the cost-benefit tradeoff of security measures, when the bulk of the evidence suggests the opposite. *The problem with the*

product we offer is not simply that it lacks attractive packaging, but that it offers poor return on investment. There are many ways to reduce potential harm with more user effort. Yet, when the answer is always "do more," they don't sound like the response to any question that the user population asks. There is a pressing need however for better protection at the same or lower levels of effort. Rather than techniques to convince users to treat low-value assets as high, we need advice and tools that are appropriate to value.

Amen.

CHAPTER 7

MAKING IT JUST WORK

When your program is ready to release, you exhaustively test the code by running it through every possible scenario.

The same needs to happen with your UX. Before releasing it to users, you need to go through a final review, to ensure that you've done everything possible to make it easy to use. This chapter provides a framework to help you do that.

The Key to Everything

As aviation pioneer Antoine de Saint-Exupéry (1900–1944) wrote, "Perfection is achieved not when there is nothing more to add, but when there is nothing left to take away." That applies to our user experiences as much as to aviation. Before we ship a product or publish a Web site, we need to ruthlessly examine it to see how much user effort we can remove.

Applications and Web sites are often feature driven. One group of users wants an equation editor, another wants a left-handed veeblefetzer, and so on. All say they want a simple and clean UX but, damn it, with *my* feature in it. The voice crying for simplicity and ease of use gets drowned out by the combination of multiple narrow interests. It's sort of like the government budget that way.

To combat this creeping complexity, what you do in the night or week or month before shipping is not to cram in one more feature, but to make another pass through the UX and ask, "How can we simplify our users' tasks even further? Make this app easier to use? And easier still?"

This chapter provides a framework to guide you along that path. Before you think about releasing to QA, you need to work through all of these items. Ideally, you should be running them throughout the development, as you run your code tests throughout your development process. But especially before release, you need to take a timeout and pay special attention to these items. If you want to think of them as Plattski's Ten Commandments, feel free:

- Start with good defaults.
- Remember everything that you should.
- Speak your users' language.
- Don't make users do your work.
- Don't let edge cases dictate the mainstream.
- Don't make the user think.
- Don't confirm.
- Do undo.
- Have the correct configurability.
- Lead the witness.

Start with Good Defaults

It's not enough to build a program with the correct feature set, or even with the correct configuration points. You also need to put that program into its optimal configuration by default, so that as many users as possible can use it without thinking. That means that you have to know

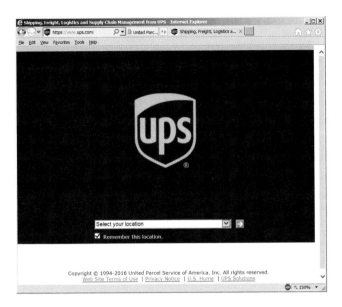

Figure 7.1   UPS.com home page requiring location choice.

who your users are, because they sure as heck aren't you. How should we determine what those default settings should be?

Sometimes you can deduce the correct default settings from your business data. Consider the UPS.com Web site discussed in the introduction, shown here as Figure 7.1. UPS forces home page visitors to select a country before they can do anything at all. This site should automatically sniff out the requesting IP address and default to the country from which it comes, as does Google, but apparently UPS won't expend even that tiny amount of programmer time. Instead, they annoy every single user by providing no default setting, by requiring them to take action.

If UPS won't deduce the user's country at runtime, here's what its second choice should be: According to UPS.com's own data, UPS's average volume is 87% domestic US and 13% international. If UPS.com defaulted to US English, seven out of eight users would be happier, and the remaining one out of eight no worse off. That sounds like a good trade-off. I doubt that the UPS designers come right out and say, "Let's annoy seven Americans so that our one annoyed foreigner won't feel lonely," but that's the result of their design choices. A hard-wired default based on business data sometimes makes sense, as it does in this case.

Sometimes you choose defaults based on usage data that you've measured from telemetry of previous versions. For example, the default toolbar in Microsoft Word 2003 contained a Quick Print button (Figure 7.2). Instead of displaying the full print dialog with all the fancy settings, this button simply printed one copy of the whole document on the default printer. But in Office

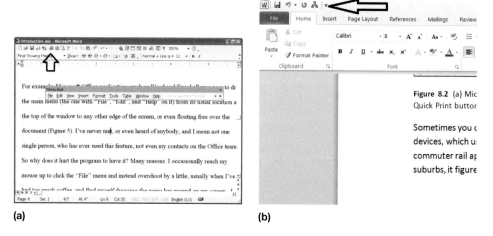

(a)   (b)

Figure 7.2   (a) Microsoft 2003 default Office toolbar containing the Quick Print button. (b) Microsoft Word 2010 quick access toolbar without the Quick Print button.

2010, the default quick access toolbar in the far upper left doesn't contain a Quick Print button, although it contains Save, Undo, and Redo (Figure 7.2b). The Quick Print button is easy to add, but it's not the default. You'd think that most users would want quick printing; therefore it should be turned on by default. If the Office team has telemetry data that proves most users don't care about quick printing, I withdraw my objection to its absence.

Sometimes you can deduce the correct default from the context of your app's usage. This is especially true of mobile devices, which often provide information based on their current location. Here's an example from the mobile phone commuter rail app discussed in the next chapter. The app senses its location when you bring it up. If it sees that it's in the suburbs, it figures you probably want to see trains inbound to the city, so it automatically selects the tab showing that schedule (Figure 7.3a). If it sees that it's in the city, it figures you probably want to see outbound trains and automatically selects the tab showing those (Figure 7.3b). That's correct for most users most of the time. And if it isn't, the user has to tap only once to see the other schedule. Just think how annoying this app would be if it asked every user, every time, "Which schedule do you want to see now, inbound or outbound?"

The best usage of default values that I've ever seen is Amazon's patented 1-Click ordering (Figure 7.4). In addition to the usual button for adding an item to a shopping cart, Amazon puts an immediate order button right there on every item's page. Just click it, and *ka-ching*! One copy of the item gets ordered, shipped to the default address by the default method, paid for by the default credit card. I had to turn this feature off because I was buying too much stuff. *That* is the power of good default values.

Always ask: Is your app using the best possible defaults?

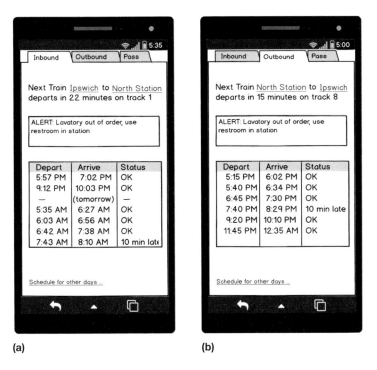

Figure 7.3 (a) The commuter rail app sees its location in the suburbs and shows the inbound schedule by default. (b) The same app sees its location in the city and shows the outbound schedule by default.

Figure 7.4 Amazon's 1-Click order mechanism, showing default settings.

Remember Everything That You Should

"I never forget a face," quipped Groucho Marx. "But in your case, I'll make an exception." That's how our programs should be. We should usually remember everything we possibly can about the last time the user used our system. There are times and places to make exceptions, for example, deliberately wiping out a browser's search history so the next user can't see the sites we visited. But almost always, our computer programs should remember the way we like things and automatically do them that way the next time we run them.

Consider the PatientSite patient portal (discussed in Chapter 9). The users of this site tend to be older than the population average, because that's who gets sick most often. Older users have poorer eyesight than the population average. PatientSite therefore provides a mechanism for increasing the text size, as do many other Web sites. Figure 7.5 shows this control.

Unfortunately, PatientSite doesn't retain this setting from one session to another. The user has to set his preferred text size with every usage. That's wrong. If a user needs large type on Monday, it's a pretty good bet that he'll need large type again on Tuesday, and probably Wednesday as well. The site should remember this setting and automatically use it on subsequent encounters.

Because of the confidentiality of its medical contents, PatientSite never shows any personal data until you have logged in. By the time it shows you this home page, PatientSite already knows who you are and has access to all of your medical data. There is no technical reason that they can't store the text size. They should do this, and so should your apps.

Figure 7.5   Text size control on the PatientSite Web site, at the top, just left of center.

note

There's a case to be made that the font size setting shouldn't be done on each Web site. The thought is that when a user needs large type on site A, he probably needs it on site B and site C as well, and all the rest of the Web too. Therefore, the correct solution is the zoom setting that all browsers have. If this type size setting were removed because of that, we couldn't squawk too much, always subject to the pro- viso of changing our minds because of actual user data. But as long as the setting exists on the site, it should persist from one session to the next.

Always ask: Is your app remembering everything that it should from one session to another?

Speak Your Users' Language

"The Internet isn't working," says my wife. So I ask her, "Won't your browser come up? Is your TCP connection valid? Is their site down?" She doesn't recognize those terms. All she knows is "the Internet," and right now it's not giving her what she wants.

Users learn about technology, as we learn everything else, by assigning names to things. Users will remember and understand the names that make sense to them. Those names often aren't the names that the developers gave these items when they built them.

One of the main problems that tech support technicians encounter is to decipher the behavior of the user's computer based on the names by which the user describes the problem. I once (many years ago) confused the living daylights out of a Dell tech support rep by continually referring to "my laptop," when all of his support material used the term "notebook" for the product I was working with.

It is not the user's job to learn the names you assign to things, even though you wish it were. It is your job to figure out the names that the user recognizes and to speak to the user in those terms.

For example, I recently went to the Web to buy some filters for my air conditioner. When I went to check out, I had to select the shipping method. Figure 7.6 shows the confusing choices that the site gave me.

Did I want "Smart Post" for $9.90? Or did I want "Home Delivery" for an additional 63 cents? What are these? Does Smart Post not go to my home? If it doesn't, how smart could it be, and where does it go instead? Of course I want it delivered to my home. And how long would either of these methods take? The checkout page doesn't tell me.

The site used the shipping company's brand names for each particular shipping service. I didn't know those names, didn't want to have to know those names, to this day *still* don't give a flying fish about those names. Even when I went poking around the Web to decipher them, and discovered that they're different flavors of FedEx, I still couldn't figure out when my package would arrive with either one. I wound up picking one at random, but I can't remember which. My stuff eventually arrived, but I wasn't sure how or when.

A far better usage is shown in Figure 7.7 with, as usual, Amazon.com. Amazon doesn't tell me which carrier will deliver my package; my Amazon stuff arrives via UPS, FedEx, USPS, once in

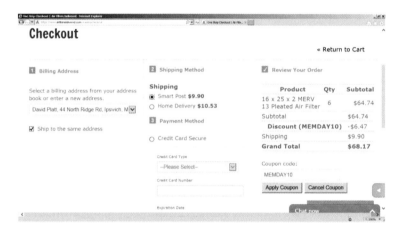

Figure 7.6   Indecipherable shipping options.

Figure 7.7   Descriptive shipping options.

a while DHL, with no discernible pattern. Amazon doesn't show me whatever brand names that carrier might use; is it UPS Blue or Red, or USPS Express Mail or Priority Mail or Priority Mail Express? Amazon presents the shipping options to me in terms of what I care about: time and cost. Free delivery in two days. Free delivery with an extra credit if I let them take five days. Or overnight for a lot more. They're speaking my language, and I can easily pick the alternative that is right for me now.

Always ask: Is your app speaking the users' language, rather than expecting the user to learn yours?

Don't Make Users Do Your Work

We see it all day, every day, in our travels through the software world: "Enter your phone number [or government ID number, or credit card number, or whatever] with no dashes or spaces." If somehow you ignore the instruction and include those placeholders, the app gets upset and won't do what you want. How annoying.

This is a classic example of forcing users to do work because programmers are too lazy to do it for them. For example, Figure 7.8 shows the Microsoft Store page for adding a credit card to an account. This isn't an old or obscure case that Microsoft just hasn't gotten around to updating yet. This is Microsoft's flagship consumer sales portal in early 2016. Microsoft is saying, "It's your job to translate your data into the format that our computer program needs. We won't do it for you. If you get it wrong, we'll show you an error message in red and say, 'Come back and do it right, you idiot.'"

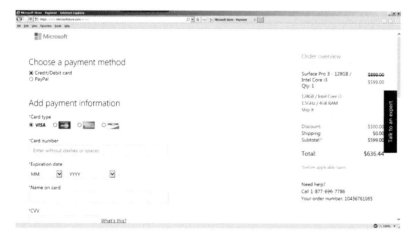

Figure 7.8   Users are forced to remove dashes or spaces from their credit card number in Microsoft Store.

Is this any way to treat a customer? It's hard to imagine how they got that one past whatever UX review they have. By definition, they must not have had a good one. What carelessness. What—please forgive me as I use the most toxic word in the geek vocabulary—stupidity.

Suppose you were talking to a human operator (remember them?), ordering from a paper catalog (remember them?), or over a voice line (remember them?). You'd start reading the card number to the operator: "Four one two six [pause] nine . . ." and she'd interrupt: "Wait! You're not allowed to pause between digits. Now go back and say it right." "I'm sorry," you say. "I'm just not with it today. OK, four one two six nine seven eight three, um," "No, you screwed it up again!" the operator screams at you. "You're obviously not telephone literate. Keep your money, we don't want any customers as stupid as you."

How long would that company stay in business? Not very long. Yet that's what Microsoft—and in fairness to them, many, *many* other sites—are doing to us today. Why do we accept this?

Apple.com does it a tiny bit better. When you type a dash or a space character into a credit card number, the text box control simply ignores that keystroke. Type in 45 67-89, and the control shows 456789. At least Apple isn't making its users do that work, though it's a little confusing when the user compares the card in his hand to the number that he typed in.

As is usual, or at least common, the prize for the best job goes to Amazon, as shown in Figure 7.9. Amazon allows the user to type in a credit card number with any sort of formatting. Put dashes or spaces in at any location you want, even if they're not shown that way on your actual card. Amazon automatically discards the chaff and assembles the card number internally.

Figure 7.9 Amazon wisely accepts credit card numbers any which way. Note the selection of Visa, which Amazon deduced automatically from the card number.

Amazon is so smart about it that it detects the type of credit card by its number, so you don't even have to tell it that.

Are Microsoft's programmers any less smart than those at Amazon? No, they're both quite good. Does Microsoft want its customers' money any less than Amazon wants its customers' money? It's hard to imagine that (although see nineteenth-century mathematician Georg Cantor's work on the different sizes of infinity). Microsoft could do this if it wanted, and it wouldn't take very long. But somehow Microsoft has not yet taken to heart the lesson that Amazon has, which is: When you want customers' money, it is a very good idea to make it as easy as possible for them to give it to you.

Always ask: Is your app making your users do work that you should be doing for them?

Don't Let Edge Cases Dictate the Mainstream

Oftentimes geeks just throw features into an app because they think they're cool, without a thorough analysis of which operations they help versus which they hinder. If pressed, the geeks insist that some user sometime might want that feature. They do not realize that a feature can easily become a cost for users who don't care about it.

Consider the case of DiscoverBulk.com, a Web site that shows you stores that sell food in bulk. Like so many retail sites, it has a store finder, shown in Figure 7.10. I typed in my zip code and

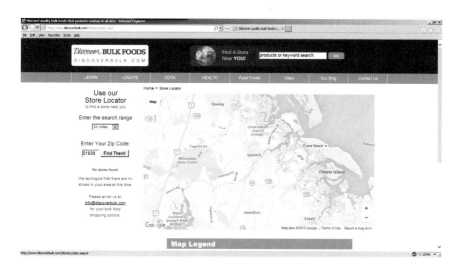

Figure 7.10   Edge case ("Is there a Discover Bulk within 20 miles?") interfering with the main case ("Where's the nearest Discover Bulk?").

clicked the "Find Them!" button. The site came back with a map of my town but the small red legend "No stores found." What's going on here?

The answer comes from the search range control, which here has the default value of 20 miles. There doesn't seem to be a store within 20 miles. If I bump it up to 50 miles, I still get no stores found. If I raise it to 100 miles, I see one in Waterboro, ME, 75 miles away.

What's wrong with this? you ask. Here's the answer: The presence of the search range control changes the question that the site answers for the user: "Is there a Discover Bulk store within 20 miles of me? How about 50?" That's not a question a user often asks.

The user almost certainly wishes to ask the question "Where's the nearest Discover Bulk store? How about the next nearest?" Users may or may not be willing to travel that far once they see where it is, but that's what they want to know, the *main case*. Locating a store within a specific radius is something that users do much less often, hence the term *edge case*. On this site, the edge case complicates the main case.

Geeks will often argue with me when I show them this sort of case, saying, "You're not willing to drive 75 miles, so this is a useful thing." The problem is that users don't know how far they're willing to go until they see how far they have to. They don't think, "Hmm, these bulk guys are somewhat interesting, but I'm willing to drive only ten miles for them. Now where the heck are they?" On the contrary: they'll see where they are, and then they'll decide what they want to do. Shut up, get out of the damn way, and show it.

Always ask: Are any of your edge cases complicating your main cases?

Don't Make the User Think

Steve Krug wrote an entire book entitled *Don't Make Me Think* (New Riders, 2014). Buy it and read it. Krug is right. Anytime you force the user to think, you are running the risk that she might not. Here's an example that happened to me.

I got a marketing email from VRBO.com, from whom I was renting a summer cottage for a week. I didn't want to keep getting marketing emails, so I looked for the unsubscribe link, which email blasters usually have. When I clicked that link, I got the page you see in Figure 7.11, asking which of its many brands I wanted them to shut up and stop bugging me about. (How about all of them?) How should I know who sent me the email? It's not my job. They sent it to me; now they need to track the damn thing. But no, they are making me guess.

I took a guess and clicked on one of them. But when I got in there, I found no indication if I was in the right place or not. The unsubscribe box wasn't checked. I can't tell if I'm subscribed to this one or not (Figure 7.12). I tried the entire top row, to see if any of them had any indications, but none did.

Figure 7.11   Unsubscription making the user think.

Figure 7.12   Unsubscription form making the user think again.

Figure 7.13   Unsubscription confirmation form making me think again, and not showing if I'm actually unsubscribed.

I eventually went through the entire top row and clicked unsubscribe for each of them. But the completion screen didn't tell me if I had actually managed to unsubscribe (Figure 7.13). Look, turkeys, when a user says shut up, it's a really good idea not to argue.

A marketingbozo (a word that I coined; see my April 2013 *MSDN* column) might argue, "But we don't want our customers to unsubscribe. We want them to stay with us, so we purposely make unsubscription hard." It's not a good idea to keep people in when they've already told you they want out. Annoying someone into liking you is extremely difficult.

Always ask: Are we making our users think?

Don't Confirm

The common technique of confirmation, popping a dialog box into the user's face and asking, "Are you sure you want to do that?" is evil (Figure 7.14). It's unfriendly, it's distracting, and it's completely ineffective. Have you ever, even once, said, "Whoa! I didn't want to do that. Thanks," and clicked No? Have you seen anyone do that? Have you even heard of anyone doing it? I haven't. It shouldn't exist. Anywhere. Ever.

We might just tolerate the annoyance of confirmation if it actually made us safe, but research has shown again and again that it does not. Confirmation is so vastly overused that it has become completely useless. Because the box constantly cries "Wolf!" like the shepherd boy in Aesop's fable, no one pays attention to it, even when it's warning you of something you really

Figure 7.14   This confirmation box does not prevent errors. The Recycle Bin, to which the file moves, makes this operation undoable and does indeed prevent unintended loss of data.

don't want to do. You cruise through it on autopilot, clicking Yes without thinking, an action the cognitive scientists call "chaining."

Other operations in life don't require confirmation. Your car does not ask, "Do you really want to start the engine?" when you turn the key. The supermarket clerk does not ask, "Do you really want to buy these?" when you place groceries on the register belt. Programmers constantly ask for confirmation because they think users don't understand the consequences of their commands. That may be true, given the poor quality of the user interface. But confirmation doesn't solve this problem. If the user was confused when he first gave whatever command triggered the confirmation box, he'll be even more confused when he sees it and almost always click Yes just to make it go away.

On the contrary, mistakenly believing that a confirmation box will prevent users from making mistakes gives programmers a false sense of security. It keeps them from having to clearly explain to the user what he's doing, and providing a way to recover when he does something that he later regrets, despite having originally confirmed it.

Legend has it that the engineers who built Amazon's astoundingly profitable 1-Click ordering mechanism originally included a confirmation box: "Are you *sure* you want to order this with 1-Click?" They fought against its removal and required a direct order from Jeff Bezos himself to remove the box and make it a true one-click process. Amazon's stock price records the value of that decision (among others, of course).

But what if the user really has made a mistake? If you brought a flashlight to the checkout stand with a package of the wrong-size batteries, wouldn't an attentive clerk ask, "Are you sure you want this size and not the one that fits the flashlight you're buying?" A good user interface should and can save us from mistakes like that, but it won't happen by blindly and stupidly asking, "Are you sure?" Instead, a good user interface prevents the problem initially by *just working*. Perhaps the Web page selling flashlights would contain a check box saying "include batteries," checked by default. Better still, the flashlight would come with batteries already inside it, so it'd work the instant you unwrapped it and no one would ever have to worry about buying the correct size. Now that's a design that just works.

Once in a while, you will get into an argument with someone at your company who outranks you and demands a confirmation box. In this case, if you are stuck putting it in, try to get permission for a check box that says, "Don't show this box again," so it doesn't nag users forever.

Always ask: Are we ever asking the user for confirmation? Because it doesn't work. We need something else.

Do Undo

Another reason that you aren't asked to confirm starting your car or buying groceries is that these operations are easy to undo. You just turn off the car or return the unwanted item. The "undo" capability is the greatest design advance since the mouse. It takes an enormous amount of effort to make this feature work so that users don't even have to think about it ("Easy is hard," the saying goes), but the programmers who implement it are any user's best friends. I buy them beer whenever I meet them.

The beauty of undo is that it allows users to explore a program. It's not always easy to understand a new program's operation from menu items and toolbar pictures. With undo, a user can try different commands, knowing that she won't damage something that can't be repaired with a few keystrokes. Programmers often regard incorrect user input as the act of an idiot who should have read the instruction manual. It isn't. It is the primary mechanism by which the human species learns.

No human being is ever 100% certain about anything; just ask anyone who's ever been married. An application with undo capability recognizes and honors a user's humanity. One that lacks undo is insisting that a user become something other than human to use that application successfully. Which would you rather buy?

The Windows Recycle Bin and its predecessor, the Apple Trash Can, are the classic examples of undo capability. Instead of a file being immediately shredded, it gets moved to a holding location from which it can be retrieved.

If undo is implemented correctly, there's only one destructive operation in the entire system: emptying the Recycle Bin. Some would say that this operation should have a confirmation box, as it currently does (Figure 7.15). But even here, the confirmation dialog exists only to guard against another bad design decision, placing the Open menu item next to Empty Recycle Bin (Figure 7.16). One slip of the mouse, sliding down two spaces instead of one, and you get the

Figure 7.15   Bad placement of the Empty Recycle Bin menu item adjacent to the Open menu item.

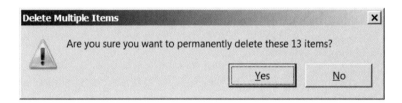

Figure 7.16   Confirmation box used to try to address bad placement of menu items.

latter instead of the former. That's bad. Emptying the Recycle Bin should have a special action used for no other purpose, perhaps clicking on it while holding down some key. Better still, the Recycle Bin should automatically delete files after some configurable period of time so you'd seldom have to empty it manually. Don't you wish that your real trash cans *just worked* like that?

Features such as the Recycle Bin work for ongoing sessions with desktop applications, but what about shorter interactions? How could, say, an Amazon 1-Click purchase be made undoable? It's actually quite ingenious. Your 1-Click order is placed into your account, but it isn't actually executed for 30 minutes after being placed. If you order something with 1-Click and then change your mind, you can just go to your orders and cancel it.

In addition to making operations undoable in the software layer, you should also think about making operations undoable in the business layer. Most merchandise can be returned to Amazon within a month, if you order something by accident or just decide you don't like it. Even Kindle digital books have a three-day free return policy, which I've sometimes used when I've tapped the wrong button by accident. Undo can extend many levels deep.

Always ask: Have I done everything that I can to make this app's actions undoable?

Non-Undoable Operations

Having just urged you to make everything undoable, there are certain categories of operations that cannot, by their very nature, be undone. Ejecting from an aircraft (Figure 7.17a) is one example, as is amputating a leg (Figure 7.17b).

Geeks often say, "Well, that means that we still need confirmations, saying, 'Are you sure?'" It is true that because of their irreversible nature that it is extremely important to ensure that we are choosing these operations correctly. That is all the more reason to get away from this idea of a confirmation box, because it does not solve this important and serious problem.

Look at the photos in Figure 7.17, and you will note that these irreversible operations fall into two categories: those that are time critical, like the ejection, and those that are not, like the amputation. Let's examine these two cases separately.

The first case, the time-critical case, is deadly. The pilot in the picture shown punched out of his F-16 less than a second before it hit the ground. He doesn't have time to deal with a confirmation box: "Are you sure you want to eject? Really sure? Really, really sure?" So the ejection has to be instantly available.

This means that the number-one thing you have to guard against is a slip—setting off the ejection seat by accident when you do something else nearby. Figure 7.18 shows a US Air Force

(a)   (b)

Figure 7.17   (a) One example of a non-undoable operation. (b) Another example.

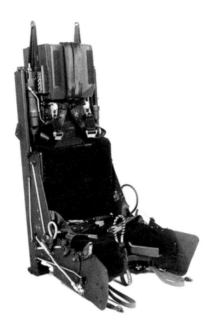

Figure 7.18   This ejection seat guards against slips by putting the handle between the pilot's legs and requiring an upward pull.

ejection seat. You can see that there's a special handle to fire it. It's distinctively marked, and it's not near anything else. The pilot has to pull it up, so a bump won't set it off (the pilot desperately hopes).

We need protection against slips in software as well. In Figure 7.15, the Empty Recycle Bin item is right next to Open. That's like putting the ejection seat handle right next to the air conditioning controls. It's way too easy to click Empty when you meant to click Open. That's why there's a confirmation dialog box for Empty—not because the user doesn't know what he's doing, but because he might have slipped into it by mistake when he was reaching for the thing next to it.

If this operation were time critical, as is ejecting from an aircraft, that wouldn't be acceptable. Instead, there would be a specific motion used for no other purpose, perhaps chording the mouse—pressing both buttons at once—on the Recycle Bin icon. That's how our familiar three-finger salute, Ctrl-Alt-Delete, was chosen. Because it rebooted the computer, trashing any work that hadn't been saved, the original designers wanted to ensure that you couldn't do it by accident. They deliberately made it a two-handed operation.

Ejecting from an aircraft is a very expensive operation. A new F-16 costs about $20 million, not counting the cost of replacing whatever it hits on the ground. The people who fly these things are very highly and expensively trained, and very few people can qualify to be an F-16 pilot.

So banging on their heads until they become more like a computer can be done, to a certain extent. Even here, aircraft piloting and management is one of the problem domains where serious study of the science of human factors got started.

Obviously, you want to try to stay away from irreversible operations that are also time critical. Think hard about your business process to minimize this set. Ejection seats for fighter pilots are one thing, but you don't want to give them to civilian airline passengers. Plan on extensive and expensive training, frequent qualifying and requalifying, and a very small user population.

Now suppose time is not critical, at least not in the split-second sense that an ejection seat is. In this case accuracy of the irreversible operation is the controlling parameter, and if it takes somewhat longer to make sure you've gotten it right, that's an acceptable trade-off. This category is much larger than the ejection seat category.

Consider the problem of wrong-site surgery. We humans have two of lots of things, such as hands and eyes, and the things of which we have only one (spines, say) generally have two sides. When a patient is draped and sedated, one anesthetized body looks a lot like the next, especially when a surgeon has worked on 12 of them already this week.

Operating on the wrong part of the patient is far more common than it ought to be. That's my favorite good-news, bad-news joke of all time: "The bad news is that we amputated the wrong leg. The good news is that your other leg is getting better after all."

A study of hand surgeons published in the February 2003 issue of the *Journal of Bone and Joint Surgery* reported that about one in 27,000 operations was performed on the wrong site. That doesn't sound like a high incidence, but with the number of operations the survey covered, that's 242 wrong-site surgeries. The right number would have been zero. You'd think a highly trained specialist hand surgeon ought to at least be able to operate on the correct body part every single time, but 21% of the responding surgeons reported operating on the wrong one at least once in their career. And if one out of five surgeons admits to it, even anonymously, a cynic cannot help but wonder how much higher the true percentage is.

So how has the medical community addressed that problem? The American Association of Orthopedic Surgeons started a program called Sign Your Site. Figure 7.19 shows one of their advertisements for it. In a preoperative meeting with the patient, the surgeon signs his initials on the operation site with an indelible marker. Ideally the patient will sign the surgical site as well. If the patient can't sign, the patient's representative does, and if that's not possible, a nurse verifies the patient record and does the signature. The hospital has protocols in place so that markings are uniform; for example, only the operative site is marked. In the operating room, the surgeon checks for the markings before starting and another member of the surgical team verifies them. The Joint Commission for the accreditation of hospitals requires such protocols for accreditation. If surgeons are willing to admit to being human and therefore fallible, and if they're willing to curtail their freedom because of it, you know the problem is serious.

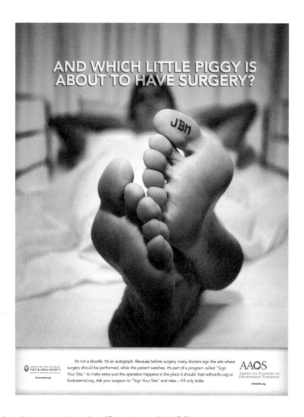

AND WHICH LITTLE PIGGY IS ABOUT TO HAVE SURGERY?

It's not a doodle. It's an autograph. Because before surgery, many doctors sign the site where surgery should be performed, while the patient watches. It's part of a program called "Sign Your Site," to make extra sure the operation happens in the place it should. Visit orthoinfo.org or footcaremd.org. Ask your surgeon to "Sign Your Site" and relax – it'll only tickle.

Figure 7.19   Signing the operation site. (Courtesy of AAOS)

Looking at these examples, what general principles do we see? I see two. First, that humans can hold only so many things in their heads at once. When the surgeon is about to start an operation, there are a lot of things running around in his head; he's worried about the operation he just did and the one he's going to do next, he's worried about leading the team and managing all the other participants, and sometimes—not often, but sometimes—he scrambles the site. When he's having a preoperative meeting with the patient, he's got a lot fewer distractions. Second, we're seeing that two heads are better than one. If both the surgeon and the patient agree on the operative site, it's much harder for the surgeon to make a mistake.

Always ask: Have I done everything possible to avoid damaging slips?

Always ask: Have I done everything possible to bring in a second head on critical operations?

Have the Correct Configurability

One of the main advantages of computerized user interfaces is that we can vary them from one user to another, to give each what she wants. It is very tempting to allow this configurability to expand, to blossom, to metastasize, until chaos results. I'm not saying that you should never make anything configurable. I'm saying think carefully about what should and what should not be configurable, always taking into account who your users are, what problems your users are trying to solve, and what they would consider to be the characteristics of a good solution.

Why shouldn't everything in the world be configurable? I always used to say that it should. "This thing is on the left, but I'd prefer it on the right. Why can't I put it there? Why can't you make it configurable? Don't tell me what I ought to want. Shut up and do what I tell you."

Excess configurability presents two problems. First, it's more expensive than you think. As a developer, you think, "Sure, no problem, just an hour or two to program this or that configurability feature." But when you implement an OR, everyone else in the development process has to implement an AND—the documentation, the tech support, the testers, the trainers, and so on. The downstream costs are enormous, at least a factor of ten higher than the initial development costs.

But even ignoring those internal economic constraints, excess configurability harms the UX. It provides the blind alleys that unsuspecting users can now stumble into, that they didn't want and that only serve the obscure edge case. A configurable thing is *not necessarily* a blessing. Compare the time wasted by everyone who mistakenly gets there against the benefit of the one guy who now has what he wants.

Because you're a geek, you probably tend to err on the side of configurability—partly because it's hard to know what users want, so you take the copout and try to give it to them both ways, and partly because, being a geek yourself, you mentally lean toward the side of configurability. It's hard to get that idea out of your head, no matter how hard you try.

There is no one-size-fits-all level of configurability that you should provide. It depends, as always, on who the user is. For example, Visual Studio, Microsoft's flagship software developer environment, is configurable to hell and back again. That's what the hyper-geeks who use it want, and Microsoft gives it to them. That's the correct and proper level there.

But overconfigurability can be harmful. Consider Figure 7.20. It shows the floating menu bar that was part of Office 2003. If you overshot in selecting the File menu, you wound up dragging the entire menu bar around on the screen. You could use it floating around, or you could dock it on the sides or bottom of the window. That was worse than useless. Have you ever seen, or even heard of, anyone who ever did that because they *wanted* to? No. It was especially bad for new users. They'd see the menu floating around, know they didn't want it, but not know how to put it back. They'd see the X at the right corner, click on it, and close the menu. It didn't go back to its initial location, it just disappeared, and now those newbies were trying to figure out Word without a main menu. That was something that should never have been made configurable.

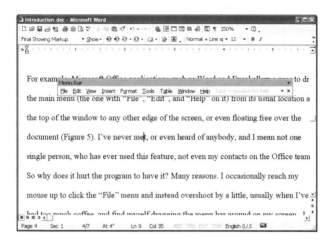

Figure 7.20 This user interface was way overconfigurable.

Figure 7.21 Amazon Kindle font face and size configurations.

At the complete opposite end are the items that represent the essence of an application, the configurability of which is absolutely critical. The classic example is the text font and size in Amazon's Kindle reader apps and devices, as shown in Figure 7.21. You open the app to read text, and choosing a comfortable font is very much the essence of the beast. Beginning readers, college students, senior citizens, and dyslexic people all need to read and all have different requirements. By including them, we increase the overall market for Kindle books and drive the virtuous adoption cycle upward.

Let's leave this issue with the following thought: If something does not need to be configurable, it *does* need to be *nonconfigurable*. Or to put it another way, if it's a toss-up, it's not a toss-up.

Always ask: Are my configuration points important for my mainstream users?

Always ask: Are my configuration points done in such a way that users won't get lost with them?

Always ask: Am I making something configurable that shouldn't be?

Lead the Witness

You've seen it on courtroom TV shows and movies: "Objection! Leading the witness." This means that the lawyer was asking questions that suggested the desired answer. That may be wrong in courtrooms, but it's 100% right in UX design.

One of the most amazing things is a program's ability to guess, under certain circumstances, what the user needs and automatically provide it. It's great, and we should do it as much as we can.

First, the bad example. Look at CNN.com, shown in Figure 7.22. If you want to search for something, you can type what you want into the search box. But that box gives you no assistance on your input. You can't see what's trending, or what others are looking for, nor do you get any assistance in spelling. If you type the search term "Red Sox," the site shows links to some stories. If you misspell it "Socks," tough noogies—you don't get the results you're looking for (unless, of course, the story is actually filed under the misspelled term, which it sometimes is).

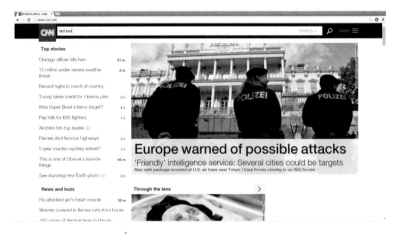

Figure 7.22   This search control provides no suggestions whatsoever.

The *New York Times* (Figure 7.23) is just a smidge better. As you start typing, it shows things starting with what you've typed; so for "Red S," it shows things like "red sun mining."

Google completely blows these guys out of the water. As you're *typing* your query, it not only shows trending searches and other people's search terms ("red sox stink"), but it's actually pre-fetching the data (see the panel on the right in Figure 7.24). There's the Red Sox logo, their manager, their championships, their roster, and so on. When there's a game on, it would show the line score of the game as it progresses, and the league standings. You haven't even finished typing what you want, and Google is providing you not with links, but with the actual data. This is absolutely amazing.

Figure 7.23 The search control gives us a few suggestions here, but not much.

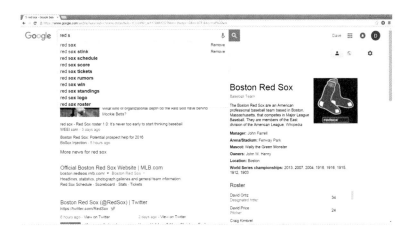

Figure 7.24 This search control gives not only suggestions as we type, but the actual data as well.

Figure 7.25   Google's mobile auto-fetch as we type in "Red Sox."

It's even more amazing in the mobile world. It's more important to do it here, because it's so much harder to type a search into a mobile device, and there's so much less space to waste on edge cases. As you type in "Red Sox," your phone fills with data that's relevant, as shown in Figure 7.25.

Always ask: Am I leading the witness as much as I can?

That's the last item in the final framework. Now let's examine its usage, and all of the steps in this book, on a couple of real-life UX case studies.

CHAPTER 8

CASE STUDY: COMMUTER RAIL MOBILE APP

Now that you've seen each UX design step individually, let's see how they all work together. In this chapter and the next, we'll do a case study on a real-world problem, applying our new skills and techniques end to end.

We'll start with a mobile phone app aimed at easing the daily grind for commuter rail riders. We'll focus on Boston's system, because we can easily find specific details and riders to work with. When we start applying what we've learned, you'll see that we can make things a whole lot better than they currently are.

Pity the Poor Commuter

The commuter rail system in the Boston area is owned by a state agency officially named the Massachusetts Bay Transportation Authority (MBTA), universally called "the T." It serves approximately 130,000 riders each weekday over ten lines, 394 miles of track, and 127 stations. It's the third-largest such system in the United States, behind New York City and Chicago, tied with Philadelphia.

The T got absolutely hammered by record snowfall in the winter of 2015. Trains were canceled, rescheduled, and canceled again, while cold riders shivered on windswept station platforms, fuming, "Where's Mussolini when we need him?" The director of the system resigned under fire, "for personal reasons." (I say she jumped while being pushed.)[1]

We can't make the trains run on time. But we can tell the riders when they actually are running—the true up-to-the-minute performance, not the wishful thinking of a paper schedule printed months before. We can smooth out our riders' lives. They'll know when to leave their homes or workplaces for the station, they won't waste time trying to catch a train that isn't running, and they'll be able to schedule their lives again.

The second need of commuter rail passengers is help with buying their tickets. They have to wait in line at the very few staffed ticket windows (fewer when the weather is bad, as the government employees stay home) or use the few available vending machines, which are always broken anyway. This extends their already-annoying commute and causes them stress. It would be great if we could make that go away too.

Can we make use of our new skills and knowledge, the steps we've seen in this book, to make their lives easier with a well-designed mobile app?

Current State of the Art

The MBTA already has a mobile app for buying tickets. The T made a great fuss over its introduction in late 2012, as the first such app in the nation. When we start examining it, we see that it doesn't help *our* users solve their own problems anywhere near as well as it could and should.

The home screen (Figure 8.1) is terrible. Most of its area is wasted. The top third shows what some graphic designer probably considered a pretty picture. The designers probably think of it as "our branding." The bottom third is completely blank.

---

1. The memory of that rail fiasco still burns in the region, even as I write these words a year later. As Howie Carr wrote in the February 24, 2016, *Boston Herald*, "The only way to stop the [Donald] Trump train now may be to turn it over to the MBTA."

Figure 8.1 MBTA mobile app home screen with wasted space and no functionality at all.

We can't *do* anything at all on the home screen. We have to leave it to accomplish anything—view a schedule, buy a ticket, see alerts that might affect our commute. They're squandering the most precious resource in any mobile app, a resource that could have helped us accomplish something that we actually cared about. Instead, they've given us a picture, a blank space that sort of balances it visually, and no functionality whatsoever. I suspect it's the art major's revenge for all those jokes ending, "Would you like fries with that?"

The purchasing and displaying of a ticket works not too badly, once you navigate to it from the home screen. Figure 8.2 shows the process. We select the stations by typing in the first few letters, and auto-complete (good) narrows the list. The app retains our most recent selection at the top of the list (also good), because almost everyone on commuter rail uses the same stations repeatedly (Figure 8.2a). We type in our credit card number, which it also remembers for the next time (also good), and the transaction is consummated (Figure 8.2b). When we're ready to ride, we tap a button to activate the ticket. It then flashes the color code of the day so the conductor knows it's valid. It also has a button that shows a bar code for readers that conductors might someday start carrying (Figure 8.2c).

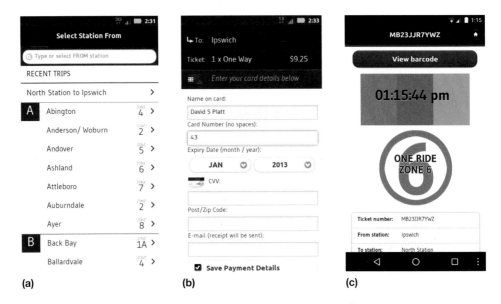

Figure 8.2 MBTA mobile app ticket purchase—not too bad.

Because it works not too badly once you get to it, we won't discuss the ticket purchase portion of this app very much. However, even with all the data it remembers, we still have to type in our credit card CVV number every time. This app is most commonly used by occasional riders, who will not have that memorized—monthly pass buyers with auto-renewal don't need it. Occasional users now have to juggle their phones and wallets and credit cards in a crowded public place, which is uncomfortable, or think ahead, which no human in the universe ever does about anything. Adding an Instant Purchase button for each recent trip at the top of Figure 8.2a, similar to Amazon's 1-Click purchase, would smooth this out even more, especially since commuters almost always travel the same route.

The app fails miserably at the greater need of commuter rail riders: accurate and timely schedule information. Again, the home screen contains no information whatsoever about schedules. If we want to see a schedule, we have to go through three steps: tapping Schedules on the home page, which then takes us to a screen where we are offered the choice between Schedules and Alerts (Figure 8.3a). The app is saying, "I know you selected Schedules, but did you really want Schedules?" After tapping Schedules again, we have to choose the line for which we want the schedule (Figure 8.3b). Only then will it show us a schedule in an ugly format that is very hard to read (Figure 8.3c).

Alerts, whatever they might be, do not appear as an option on the home page. We have to somehow intuit their existence and go digging—tap Schedules, then tap Alerts (Figure 8.3a), then look at our line to see if it has any (Figure 8.4a). The green check mark would seem to indicate that everything is OK, but despite this indicator, the Lowell line has one Upcoming alert

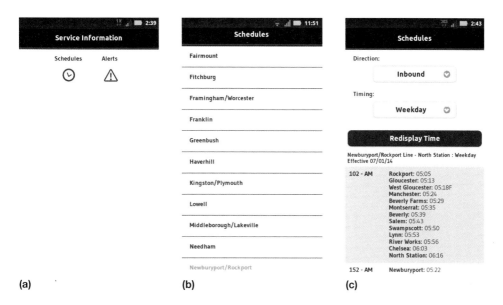

(a)   (b)   (c)

Figure 8.3   Schedules are difficult to find, then difficult to read once we've found them.

and one Ongoing alert. (What the hell is the difference between Upcoming and Ongoing? I can't tell, and when I look at the contents of each, they appear to be identical.)

If something is important enough to be called an alert ("an alarm or other signal of danger"), it surely shouldn't be buried four screens deep, should it? And isn't an "ongoing alert" a contradiction in terms? Once we look at the alert, we can see that it often impacts the schedule; note the two canceled trains (Figure 8.4b). Burying this information four levels deep ensures that no one will ever see it—exactly the opposite of what alerts are for.

The developers of the schedule portion of this app did not apply the skills that they (sort of) demonstrated in the ticket purchase portion. They didn't work from the users' perspective. They just took their paper schedules and tossed them into an app, with the awful results you would expect from such an unthinking approach.

The user has to do far more work than she should have to. The app doesn't make use of the knowledge it has about the user, or about the repetitive nature of the commuter rail relationship. The developers are saying, "Hey, it's *your* job to do all this work." Maybe that attitude was acceptable a decade ago, but it sure isn't today. If a student of mine turned in something like this, I'd flunk him so fast he'd switch his major to English.

We can do a whole lot better by following the Platt UX Protocol, putting ourselves in the users' shoes. Once we think about who the users really are and what these users actually need, we can select the items of information most relevant to them, here and now, and present them clearly and easily. That will turn this commuter rail app from a brick into an indispensable everyday aid.

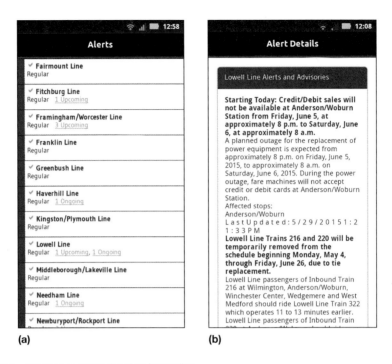

(a)   **(b)**

Figure 8.4   We have to select the alert for our line.

Step 1: Who?

Your first impulse, of course, is to bring up Xamarin and start dragging and dropping components onto the design surface. I hope this book has shown you that that's wrong. That's what the MBTA's developers probably did when they wrote this app, and look where it got them: publicly hammered in this book. Let's run the Platt UX Protocol on it and see where it takes us.

To begin: Who rides the commuter rail in Boston? What's our potential user population? Your immediate response is to shout, "Everyone; it's public transport." But you should know better than that by now.

The basic demographic information is easy to find. A quick search on the MBTA's Web site for the term *advertising* gave me the contact info for the company that manages the advertisements on the T's vehicles and stations. I emailed them for a customer kit about advertising on commuter rail and received it within the hour. It contained the basic demographics we need to get started. You can see an excerpt in Figure 8.5.

Commuter rail riders are just about evenly divided in gender, 52% male and 48% female. Commuter rail passengers skew older than the general populace. The largest single cohort is age 45 to 54, constituting 30% of ridership. Seventy-three percent of riders are age 35 or older. We could speculate that's because younger people don't move out to the suburbs until they

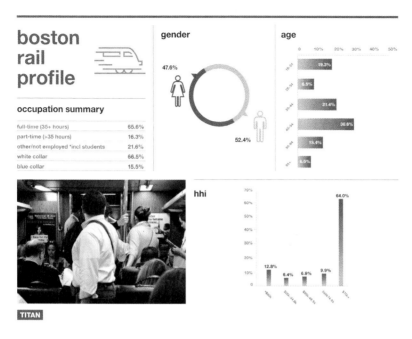

Figure 8.5   Media kit with commuter rail demographics. (Courtesy of MBTA)

marry and need room for the second kid and the swing set and the golden retriever. So no, it's not everyone. Our user population contains very few kids, and not many millennials. Our users didn't grow up with smartphones. They are not the kinds of people who say, "Way cool" when they see, for example, Snapchat. They will always speak geek with an accent.

Well, if they're that old, do they use smartphones at all? Are we barking up the wrong tree completely with the notion of any smartphone app? Fortunately, no. A quick Google search finds the *Boston Globe*'s coverage of the MBTA ticketing app initial rollout, reporting that 76% of commuter rail riders carry smartphones. That was written in 2012, and I doubt the percentage has gone down since then. We have market penetration, if we can provide customers with what they need.

Now that we have basic information about our user population—evenly split in gender, but skewing older and hence less technophilic—let's create personas to communicate that information to our development team. I worked up two personas, one who travels every workday and one who travels occasionally.

Claire (Figure 8.6) lives in Salem, Massachusetts. (You can download her full persona from this book's Web site.) She's 42, divorced, with three kids (16, 14, nine) still at home. She works at Massachusetts General Hospital as a respiratory therapy aide, on a regular eight-to-four weekday schedule. She depends on commuter rail to get herself to work every day. Commuting on buses and the subway would take her three times as long, and those kids of hers don't leave her a free

Figure 8.6 Claire, who rides the MBTA commuter rail every day to work in Boston.

minute. Driving in Boston's killer traffic at those peak times would be awful. And parking downtown costs $30 a day, which would take a huge bite out of her $18-per-hour pay.

Claire drives to the Salem commuter rail station every day and takes the 6:43 a.m. train to North Station, arriving at 7:18. She then walks or takes a shuttle bus to Mass General. She likes to take the 4:20 p.m. train home, arriving at 4:53, but often she can't get out from work in time. Then she takes the 4:45 train, arriving at 5:16. She knows the train times very well because she takes the train every day.

Her biggest headache is when the train schedule gets disrupted. It's not just snow—lightning, construction, the old equipment breaking down, vehicle accidents at a grade crossing; anything can mess it up. She doesn't know when she has to get to the station, or when to tell her family she'll be home.

Claire pays her fare with a monthly pass. Her employer kicks in 25% of it as a fringe benefit. Her phone is a four-year-old Android on a T-Mobile family plan because it's cheap.

For our second persona, I need to tell you of a Boston legend. A hypothetical man on Boston-area transit is always named Charlie, harking back to the Kingston Trio's 1959 smash hit "Charlie on the MTA," a song about a rider who never returned. Google it; it's good.

Figure 8.7   Charlie, who rides the MBTA commuter rail into Boston 25 or 30 times per year. (Photo by redjar on Flickr)

Charlie (Figure 8.7) lives in Ipswich, Massachusetts, on the same rail line as Claire, another half-hour farther out. (You can also download his persona from this book's Web site.) He is 56 and married, one child graduated from college and another halfway through, but he hasn't downsized his house yet. He is a higher-end computer consultant who sometimes works with clients in downtown Boston.

Charlie makes 25 or 30 trips per year on commuter rail. They tend to come in bunches, perhaps four trips this week and three the next, followed by several months with none. His billing rate is high enough that he could afford to drive and park in Boston, but the traffic drives him batty. He'd have to leave his house at 5:00 a.m. to beat it, and his clients don't usually like to start that early. He's happy to ride the train, drink coffee, listen to classical music on his iPod, and review the upcoming day's material on his MacBook Air. On the way home, he turns off his phone and reads a book, sometimes drinking a beer (which the conductors wink at if he keeps it in a paper bag).

He drives from his house to the commuter rail station in Ipswich. He usually takes the 7:13 a.m. train in, arriving at North Station at 8:10. He then walks or takes the subway to his client. His default return trip leaves at 5:15 p.m., arriving at 6:07. But sometimes he finishes earlier and catches an earlier train. And sometimes he has to work later, or stay in town to socialize with clients, and catches a later train. He can't remember the train times from one trip to the next because he doesn't take trains frequently enough.

Charlie usually has to buy his tickets aboard the train for cash. There's no store near his house that sells them, and no vending machine at his station. That means he has to remember to stop at the ATM and take out a $20 bill every day for his round trip. The conductor punches out a paper ticket and gives him $1.50 change. (How nineteenth century.) He has to keep the paper receipt for his expenses and manually enter it into Quicken. He could buy several from the ticket window at the main station when he gets in, but waiting in that line at rush hour is way more trouble than it's worth.

Charlie always carries the latest iPhone from Apple. He justifies the cost by saying he has to project a tech-savvy image to his clients. But he really just likes Apple stuff. He won't camp out on the sidewalk the night before a new release, but he will pre-order it from Apple's Web site.

Note that neither of our personas is a tourist or a foreign visitor, someone new to Boston. If we were dealing with buses and subways, we would definitely want to include them. But commuter rail reaches a very different audience—more homogeneous, more suburban, more repetitive. (It also makes this example much easier.)

Step 2: What (and When, and Where, and Why)?

What problems do Claire and Charlie need to solve, and what would they consider to be the characteristics of a good solution?

Riding the commuter rail is a repetitive kind of thing. Almost everyone travels from an outlying station into the city in the morning and returns to that same station in the evening. Our app needs to recognize and cater to this repetitive behavior.

It's rare that a user will change stations, even more rare that he will change the line on which he travels. It happens occasionally—a guy will stay over at his girlfriend's house and take a different train the next day—but not often. Our app needs to be able to handle changes, and make them as easy as possible on that user, but not at the cost of complicating the much more common case of "same old, same old."

What do commuter rail riders need? More than anything else, they need to know when the trains will actually leave the station. Commuter rail is not like the subway or bus that comes along every few minutes. Commuter rail trains run every half an hour during peak times, and less frequently (an hour or two, sometimes longer) outside them. If you miss one, you might wait quite a while for the next one, and the stations (particularly inbound) are not at all comfortable.

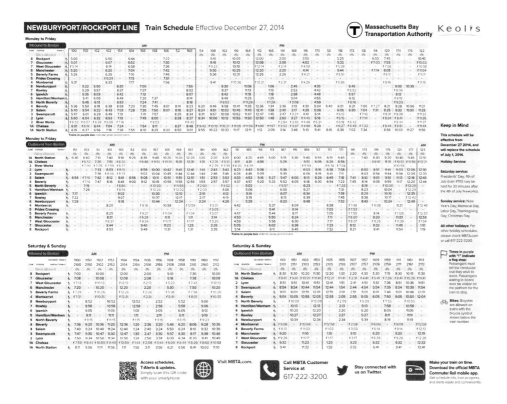

Figure 8.8 Confusing, inconvenient printed timetable. (Courtesy of MBTA)

How do riders know the schedule? Historically, the railroad has issued a printed timetable for each line (Figure 8.8). Riders have to pick up a copy, usually at the main station (where they've got scads for every line but yours), carry it with them, and then remember where they've put it and how to refold it. It's inconvenient to read, because it covers all stations on a train line and you have to pick your specific station out of it. Charlie does this every time he travels, and it's a pain. "The signal-to-noise ratio is low," he says. (Geek.)

It is not unusual that the rail schedule gets disrupted by weather or accidents or mechanical difficulties. Sometimes the delay affects just one line (a train on the Fitchburg line hits a truck), sometimes it's all of them (a presidential visit snarls the entire downtown). Riders need to know about this so they can take an earlier train to work, or drive in if they have to, or pretend to work from home, or say, "To hell with it" and fake a case of smallpox to take a sick day. Obviously the paper schedule can't tell us this.

The MBTA Web site could, but it has to cover an enormous array of topics—bus, subway, boat, and so on. It's difficult to find the specific current information that you need even with a full-size Web browser on a PC. And we often don't have access to a PC, for example, while we're waiting on the suburban platform in blowing snow for a train that isn't there. It's almost impossible to use the MBTA site on the limited area of a mobile phone.

Riders also need help buying their tickets. A quick Google search finds that 57% buy monthly passes. The rest have a quandary. Most trips originate in the suburbs. Very few suburban stations today have staffed ticket windows, or even vending machines. Once in a while a nearby store will sell tickets as a convenience, but that's increasingly rare. That was traditionally the domain of the local tobacco shop, where the riders would also pick up a newspaper and a pack of smokes for the ride. Those shops are just about all out of business today, along with the newspapers and the smokers. So most non-monthly-pass riders have to pay cash to the conductor on board. It would be nice to be able to buy tickets on demand, with credit cards.

Now that I had some handle on the problems that Claire and Charlie need to solve, I needed to ask other riders what they thought about the app. I needed to do this quickly, so I went to my local commuter rail station on a weekday morning and interviewed as many people as I could. Here's what I said to them:

- Tell me about your ride today.
- What burns you the most about it?
- How do you pay for your train ride?
- What kind of smartphone do you have?

Note that I started with open-ended questions and moved toward more specific ones. Above all, I needed these interviews to be quick. The riders start gathering at the station only about ten minutes before the train arrives, and I needed to talk to as many as I could.

I found that most of the riders complained about not enough trains, because of cancellations. (We can't really help them with that one.) Their second complaint, almost universal, was not knowing when the trains were running. They were angriest about the times the MBTA gave out wrong information. The Web site would say that a train was on time, the riders would go to the station, and the train didn't come. They wait 15 minutes, half an hour, in their cars with the engines running; still no train. The electronic sign at the station claims that the train's on time, but in reality it's been canceled and the one behind it is two hours late and packed to the gills. While our app can provide the users with the information that they need, efficiently and in a pleasing format, we can't repeal the zeroth law of computer science: "Garbage in, garbage out." Our app is only as good as the information that the MBTA gives us to feed to it.

Hardly anybody talked about buying tickets. That wasn't on their minds when I did this research. It might increase in importance as schedules returned to more normal conditions, but the riders weren't thinking about ticket purchases when I asked them.

Riders look at schedules more often than they deal with tickets. Charlie buys a round-trip ticket once per day when he travels. Claire sets up a monthly pass with auto-renewal and then doesn't touch it again. They display their tickets to the conductor once per trip, or twice per day, often not even that when the train is so crowded the conductor can't get through to check. But they look at the schedule a lot: at least once or twice the night before, the same again in the morning, and the same again in the afternoon. Charlie will probably check it more often per day than Claire, who can settle into a routine. But they both need to know about any service disruptions.

So here's what our users, Charlie and Claire, need:

- Good, up-to-the-minute schedule info, including any changes
- Good, easy ticket purchase and display
- And all of it easy, easy, easy to use

Now that I knew what users needed, I started writing it up in the form of stories so that the geeks who would code this app can understand. Here's what I wrote:

Story 1

Claire is at home in the evening, getting ready for work tomorrow. She doesn't know what's up with that stupid commuter rail schedule, due to all the snow they've had lately. She needs to know when the trains are running tomorrow, so she can know when to set her alarm for. She pulls out her Android phone, taps our app. The app sees that it's evening and that she's currently located in the suburbs. It knows from the pass she's purchased which stations she travels from and to. So it automatically comes up showing the trains inbound from that station for tomorrow morning. (She can change that with a few taps in case it's wrong, but it usually isn't.) The app says that everything's currently on schedule for tomorrow, but Claire doesn't believe that for a microsecond. She sighs and wishes she could get a job locally and not have to deal with this damn commute. But she's got seniority at her current job, her kids are headed toward college—she's stuck with it for the foreseeable future. She sets her alarm clock early anyway and goes to bed.

Story 2

Charlie is at work in downtown Boston and his client invites him to stay in town for dinner. Of course he'd love to socialize with his client; that's how he often hears about new business coming down the pipe. He needs to know the last trains of the day, so he knows when he has to leave his social engagement. He pulls out his latest iPhone (his customer's eyes widen with longing) and taps our app. The app sees that it's late afternoon, and its current location is in the city. So it automatically comes up with the outbound trains highlighted. It knows from the ticket he purchased this morning where he's traveling to, so it shows the times for that line.

There's a train leaving North Station at 7:40 p.m.; that's probably too early. He'd have to eat too fast and probably wouldn't get around to the business discussion over coffee and brandy. The next one's at 9:20, so he has time for a good outing. But the one after that leaves at 11:45. If he misses the 9:20, he'll have to sit in North Station for two and a half hours—no fun at all. And if he misses the 11:45 train, he'll have to take a $100 cab ride out to Ipswich, or sleep on the station benches. Charlie knows what his parameters are and goes off to his dinner meeting with confidence.

Story 3

Claire wakes up in the morning and turns on the coffeemaker. She looks out the window and sees some new snow. Damn! She pulls her phone off the charger, taps our app, checks to see if the train schedule has gotten even more screwed up. Double damn! It has! They canceled her regular train, but there's an earlier one (actually an even earlier one that got delayed) that she can still grab if she hustles. She yells to her older daughter that she'll have to get the younger ones out to the school bus, throws on her clothes, and runs out the door cursing the politicians who screwed up the transport network. But she makes her train, keeps her job, doesn't even get her pay docked. She does have to pick up the load for employees who couldn't get in until noon because they didn't have our great app to warn them when their trains got screwed up. Fortunately, many of the patients got stranded, too, and missed their appointments, so the workload wasn't quite as bad as it might have been. The outbound trains are also messed up, but at least she can see which ones are running. She'll order pizza delivery for dinner tonight.

Story 4

Charlie needs to buy a ticket every time he takes the train in. There isn't a ticket outlet near his stop. He used to need a $20 bill every day to buy it on board from the conductor. But now Charlie takes out his phone, taps our app, and buys a ticket, which he displays to the conductor. The bill goes to his credit card and appears magically under the "Travel" category when he downloads his transactions into Quicken. Charlie's accountant is happy. Charlie is happy. The MBTA bean counters, who want to go cashless as soon as the politicians will let them, are happy too. The world is a better place all around.

Step 3: How?

Now that we know who our users are and what they need to do, we'll start addressing how they can do it. We'll use Balsamiq to make some quick mockups based on our initial research, show them to users, and get feedback. We won't spend any time at all making them pretty. As I've said throughout this book, the key point at this stage is to iterate quickly. Polishing the cannonball is counterproductive.

The operation that users do most often is to check schedules, both promised and actual. Four or five times per day is not unusual. The more the users perceive that the schedule is likely to change, the more frequently they'll check it. So the more critical this piece is, the more critical it becomes. It's important to get it right.

The next most common thing users do is to display a ticket to the conductor. Buying is less common. Claire sets it up once in her life and the pass continues forever. Charlie does it on days he takes the train in, usually buying a round-trip, which means he does this just once per day.

We want to minimize the number of touches that the user has to make. The original MBTA app does not do that, and it never seems to have occurred to its developers that they should try. Let's take the app's knowledge of the repetitive patterns of most commuter rail users and leverage it to the max.

I made my best initial guesses based on what my live users had told me, and on what Claire and Charlie said when they disturbed my dreams at night. Figure 8.9 shows my first mockups.

I started by trying to fit everything onto just one page. In direct contrast to the MBTA app where the home page does nothing at all, this home page does everything. We don't need any

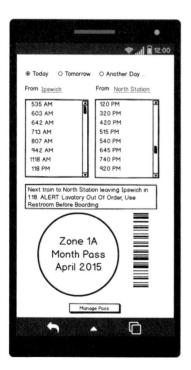
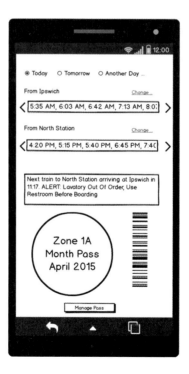

Figure 8.9 Two ideas for our first iteration of the MBTA mobile app.

navigation because we never have to go anywhere else for schedules or alerts or ticket display. Purchasing a ticket or pass requires another screen, for which we provide a button, but as I said before, this is much less common.

The first thing we see at the top is a line of three radio buttons. Users check schedules at three main times during the day: in the morning before they head out from home to the station, in the afternoon before they head out from work to the station, and in the evening at home, to see what's up for the next day. So perhaps two times out of three they want to see the current day's schedule, but in the evening they want to see the next day's schedule. The app automatically figures out which one to show, based on the time of day and the user's cell-level location. (That's precise enough for our needs and draws no extra power.) The selected radio button displays the current choice. If the user sees yesterday and needs today, or vice versa, she just taps the radio button that she wants. If she needs to see another day, perhaps on the weekend to go into town for a show, picking "Another Day" brings up a date picker to specify that date.

Next, we see the inbound and outbound trains. Here's the key improvement over the original app: because the app knows the ticket that the user bought, it knows which trains and which times to show. Claire bought a pass originating in Salem. Charlie's tickets originated in Ipswich. Both specified North Station as their destination. The app uses this knowledge to populate the labels above the list boxes and the train times within them, with the next available train at the top. Each station has a link to change it if needed. That feature likely will not get used much, but telemetry (next section) will tell us if we're wrong.

I tried two different approaches to displaying the train times. Figure 8.9a uses list boxes, displaying the train times in a vertical arrangement that the user is probably familiar with. In Figure 8.9b, I saved space by putting train times in a horizontal line. The app automatically places the next available train as the first in the list. Either scroll bars or horizontal arrows indicate to the user that she can scroll them if she needs to see more trains than fit in that space.

The app doesn't show the trains' arrival times. I figured most commuters probably wouldn't care. They know approximately how long their train ride takes and can therefore easily extrapolate. Plus, arrival time is often affected by factors beyond the rider's control, so it doesn't much matter what the schedule says. If needed, we could make train arrival information accessible with a tap on a particular train. I wonder how many users would say they need that.

Below the train displays is a text box. This carries a countdown clock, showing the time to the next train inbound (if the user is in the suburbs) or outbound (if the user is in the city). The users won't have to do mental subtraction to see if they can make that train. This text box also shows any alerts pertaining to this line or their station. Users won't have to tap down three levels to find out if there's anything they care about.

Below all this is the monthly pass or ticket display. Claire's automatically updates every day to show the correct color for validity. Charlie will have to explicitly activate one, using a button (not shown).

The main drawback with this layout is that it's a little bit cramped. Ideally it won't bother our user population much. In a reader app that they'd use for half an hour or more at a time, that would be a deal breaker, but they'll look at this app for no more than ten or 20 seconds at a pop. The main criterion was for users to be able to pick out immediately the data that they need. I carefully selected everything users needed (or so I thought), and nothing that they didn't (ditto).

The point is not that this layout is perfect, or even very good. This is my first draft. The point is that it didn't take long to dummy up these layouts *and try them on actual users*, to see what they liked and what they didn't like. To that trial we now turn our attention.

Step 4: Try It Out

I next needed to ask a number of users if they'd look at my app. I emailed my student list, asking for anyone who rode commuter rail and wouldn't mind taking a look. Obviously, this selection has a certain amount of skew. My students tend to be younger than the average rider, although since I teach in the continuing education division, they're not undergrads. They tend to be better educated than the majority of commuter rail users, although here in the Boston area we have more college grads than most places. All of them did explicitly identify themselves as commuter rail users, either current or recent, so they do know what they themselves need.

If I were going to invest major money in this mobile app, I'd need real users. I'd probably hand out cards at the commuter rail station offering $20 to any rider who'd do a half-hour Skype call to look at the app. I'd get as many riders as I wanted. Again, at this stage, I need to move quickly, so I'm thinking fewer test users rather than more. I decided to go with Steve Krug's suggestion of three. If all three of them like something, it's probably pretty good, and if all three of them hate something, it's probably pretty bad.

I arranged Skype calls with three of my former students who are regular commuter rail riders. They know me and aren't afraid to call 'em as they see 'em. Once we got our Skype session established, we chatted a little bit about their current activities to break the ice and get the conversation flowing, and then I started with open-ended prompts such as "Tell me about your commute." Then I read them the blurb from Chapter 4, how "We're not testing you. You cannot possibly make a mistake here. We're checking how well *our* software fits what you're trying to do."

I used Story 3 above, the one about Claire waking up in the morning. I figured it was the most critical one. I read it to the test subject, substituting his name for hers: "Imagine, John, that you've woken up at five in the morning to get ready for your day. You're sipping your first cup of coffee and you look out the window and damn, it's snowed six inches. You figure you had better check and see how the trains are running. You pull out your phone, tap the icon [now I share the screen in Balsamiq], and here's what you see. What do you do now?"

One of the users started talking out loud as she thought, which is helpful. I had to prompt the other two to get them started: "John, it would be really helpful if you could maybe speak out loud as you are thinking. You're obviously figuring something out; could you maybe tell me about it?" and so on.

I won't repeat the conversations verbatim, but here is a summary of what I found. The first thing every user noticed was the set of radio buttons showing Today/Tomorrow/Other. I thought those buttons were important, but the users didn't know what to make of them. I said, "OK, no problem, ignore them for now and continue. What are you thinking?" If these buttons had been a real problem, if they were too distracting to continue this test, I could have easily removed them from the Balsamiq mockup, but these users were happy enough continuing on.

They started looking at the departure times in the left list box. All of them said that they would find the one that they wanted to take and tap on it, expecting to see information about that train. I had expected the departure time to be all the information that the user needed, but these users didn't see it that way. They wanted to see the arrival time, and they wanted some sort of indicator to know if it really was on time.

Two of the three noticed the countdown timer and alerts box and understood what it was. It's a little harder to notice here in the static mockup, because in a real app you would see the time counting down and that would give a clue to its purpose. The third subject didn't notice it at first but understood it immediately when I asked him to look at it.

This was all great feedback. I thought initially that the users would not care about the arrival time, because they already knew how long the train ride takes. That wasn't the case. They all wanted to see it when making their choice of trains. They didn't want to have to add it mentally; they wanted that information in tandem with the departure times, perhaps to go to the same place in their brains. Also, they said that they didn't care about seeing the evening return trains at this point. They'd look at return trains in the afternoon when they were thinking of heading home. The return trains weren't horribly distracting, but they weren't the slightest help right then either, and their real estate could be used for something else that users cared about.

They all preferred the vertical arrangement of trains in Figure 8.9a to the horizontal line in Figure 8.9b. That's how they're shown in the timetable, that's how they're shown on the monitor in the station, and the testers found it confusing to view them otherwise. No one liked the horizontal line. OK, no problem; I learned something else.

They all said that the layout was too cramped, making it too hard to pick out the thing that they needed. In my zeal to get rid of all the navigation, I had crammed too much into one place and made the user do work of a different sort. Clearly, I hadn't found the optimax yet.

Was I angry that a bunch of idiots couldn't see the brilliance of the design? Did I scream to the heavens demanding to know how I had gotten such a brain-damaged set of test users? On the contrary. They told me things I didn't know. They made this app better. They made me smarter. And now you too, I hope.

So back I went to Balsamiq. I split this information into two different screens, with the easiest possible navigation between them. The hamburger control is popular in mobile apps, but this app has such a small amount of navigation that the extra tap it would require (tap the hamburger to see the choices, then tap the choice you want) would have been cumbersome. Instead, I used a tab control for its visible navigation. The amount of screen real estate it consumes is small compared to the benefit of instant and obvious access to this small number of choices. I put the schedule on one tab and the ticket or pass on another. You can see it in Figure 8.10.

The test users liked this one much better. They all said it was way easier to find the times that they wanted. They didn't have to tap on anything to see the arrival times. "That table, that's how they're shown on the monitor in the station, so it's really familiar," said one, and the others

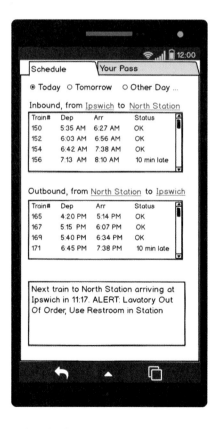

Figure 8.10 Second iteration of the MBTA mobile app, incorporating feedback from the first attempt.

agreed when I asked them. "We never use the train number at all. We always think of them as departure time, like the 8:57 train. So you might as well get rid of the column." The other users, when I asked them, said that no, they never used it either and agreed we might as well get rid of it.

They loved the tab control for navigation. I thought it might be more of a PC-based idiom, not so much for mobile phones, but they all grabbed onto it right away. Maybe it's the fact that the test users are older and more used to PCs, but then so are the actual commuter rail riders. The only disagreement was over where the tabs should go. At the top, as I originally showed? One tester wanted them at the bottom so he could select the tab with the thumb of his hand that held the phone, convenient when the train got crowded. I decided to keep them on top for now. It's not a huge deal one way or the other. That choice can easily be made in further refinements, and if we really need it both ways, we could make it configurable.

Again I encountered the desire for separation of morning inbound train times and afternoon outbound train times. Every test user said, "Better, but I still have to tell one table from another. It's easier than the first one you showed us, but why not have each in a separate tab?"

Finally, I asked each tester about the alert and countdown timer box. One said that the countdown timer was extremely important, as it told her when she had to run to make her next train. She wanted it on top for that reason. It would be nice to have the track number on it as well, if we were able to get that. That's the sort of information you will get only from conversations with your users. Telemetry can't tell you that.

Again I went back and made the changes suggested by the test users. They had said they were happy with tab navigation. They can see all the choices at once, and it takes only one tap to select any of them. They didn't care about having inbound and outbound on the same screen, so I decided to place each on a separate tab.

I moved the countdown timer to the top. Only one test user had specifically requested that, but the others all said they liked it when they saw this design.

I used the extra space on the tab to show more trains, and to make the font larger for easier reading. Think about the demographics. Half of the users are age 45 and over. The developer community skews much younger than this. It is common for them to dismiss the need for larger type as a special need; it's not the main thing, so we'll get to it when we can—definitely not version 1, probably not version 2 either, maybe version 3, or then again maybe not. But age-related presbyopia (farsightedness) begins around age 40. At least half of our user base would appreciate something easier to read. You can't call half the user population an obscure special case. They need relaxed-fit text as they need relaxed-fit jeans. They probably aren't happy about needing it, but they'd sure appreciate having it. The third tab made reading easier for everyone. The users' requirements are now working together toward the optimal solution. The result is shown in Figure 8.11.

Figure 8.11   Third iteration of the MBTA mobile app, incorporating feedback from previous attempts.

I'm still stuck on the case of Charlie sitting at home Sunday night, needing to take the train in on Monday and wondering what the schedule will be. That was the point of the radio buttons in the original mockup, which all the test users hated. But we don't want Charlie to do any additional work by having to click the Schedule for Other Days link. So I brought in a pattern I see in airports. When the monitor lists flights by time, at the end of the day when there aren't many left, they show a little banner after the last of tonight's flights, and then they start showing tomorrow's flights. So we can easily see that we're at the end of today and what's happening first thing tomorrow. I made a small change and came up with the iteration shown in Figure 8.12.

The app would be smart enough to bring up the correct tab based on the user's location. If Charlie opened it while downtown, it would figure he's most likely headed home, so it would bring up the outbound tab. Story 2 discusses this. But if Charlie opens the app in the suburbs in the evening, it would automatically show the inbound tab, with the last of today's inbound trains (if any) and the first of tomorrow's inbound trains. All the users loved this when I showed it to them.

Some other ideas surfaced here as well. One tester said, "What about a space for ads?" Much as I'd personally hate to see them, the rail agency could charge a lot of money for delivering this

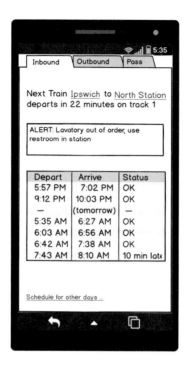

Figure 8.12 Fourth iteration of the MBTA mobile app, automatically showing tomorrow's trains at the end of the day.

clientele to advertisers, especially if it were location based and time based. Imagine that you're walking toward the station and your phone beeps. "I see you have an extra ten minutes. Here's a coupon for a free donut with purchase of a coffee at Dunkin' Donuts." Or whatever.

There was some discussion about phone-level alerts or text messages when the schedule got seriously messed up, not just notifications within the app. Interestingly, all three test users expressed a desire for some information as to how crowded a train was. After further discussion, we judged these to be impractical, as you don't know for sure how crowded a train will be until it fills up around departure time. Also, regular commuters usually know which trains are the most crowded. And there's not much they can do about a crowded train anyway.

The point of this discussion is not to learn how to make your first design perfect. Your first design will *never* be perfect. It probably won't even be all that great; mine wasn't. It is meant to stimulate discussion, to get users thinking and talking to you. You need to iterate, and therefore you need to iterate as quickly and cheaply as possible. It shouldn't take more than a week to go from sketches to testing and iterations. Lather, rinse, repeat.

There will be more detailed design, and better graphic design, as we continue development. But the point is that rapid sketching and quick feedback give us huge, *huge* advantages very quickly and very cheaply. We were able to switch designs before we'd spent much money, or much time, or gotten emotionally invested in any design. As I put on the shoes of my users, I learned all sorts of things that I never knew that I never knew. Now I know them, and so do you.

Step 5: Telemetry Plan

Every modern app uses telemetry. What will we record with our telemetry in this MBTA commuter rail mobile app, and what use will we make of that information?

In order for our app to provide the seamless capabilities we are asking of it, we need to make steadily better guesses as to what the users want. As you have seen, much of our logic is based on the time of day and the location at which the user makes requests. For example, when the user looks at the schedule in the morning in the suburbs, we deduce that he wants to see the inbound trains and come up with that tab showing. If he's in the city in the morning, he probably has a reverse commute, or pulled an all-nighter, so we bring up the morning outbound trains.

For each UX event, we need to record the time of day and the location of the phone. We won't use GPS location because of the power drain, and also potential privacy problems. But cell-level location, easily available on all phones, will serve well enough for our needs. We won't be able to tell if the user looks at our app on First Street versus Second Street. But we'll certainly know if the guy is in Salem or in downtown Boston.

The first thing most telemetry focuses on is the feature usage profile. How often do users use each feature? We went to a great deal of trouble to figure out which schedule tab to show. Did we get it right? How often do users change it? We make our best guess as to which trains to show in the schedule displays. How often do users scroll? We infer the station from the tickets the user purchases. How often does anyone change it? Does anyone ever use the Schedule for Other Days link?

Since we're selling tickets with this app, we'll want to know how often that feature gets used. We can compare that data against other channels. What percentage of monthly pass users do as Claire did, setting up her monthly pass on a Web browser on her PC, versus doing it on her phone? How many tickets does Charlie buy at a time? At what time of day does Charlie buy his tickets, and what is the peak load?

We'd learn a lot from this feature tracking. We probably shouldn't go any further until we've digested this amount of data and iterated our UX a few times based on it. We can then evolve it to almost anything we care about. Our data miners will certainly have their requests.

If we really wanted to get fancy, we could gather data from the phone's accelerometer, compare it with location and time, and figure out how often anyone ever runs for a train.

Step 6: Security and Privacy Plan

Now we come to the security and privacy plan. At first glance, this app has very little security or privacy need. All of the data on the schedule side is public. You do not need to authenticate if you want to know when the next train is arriving. There's not a whole lot to be concerned with.

Certainly someone who steals the phone can see which train line the user has been looking at, and it's a pretty good bet that's the one she's been riding all along. A user has far worse things to worry about if her phone gets stolen, like the content of her text messages. A user will secure almost anything else, even her Kindle reading list, before she cares about locking up her train schedule. If a user does worry about her commuter rail profile becoming public, she'll get a phone that encrypts its entire contents and locks it all up with a fingerprint reader.

The only piece that needs to be secure is the credit card number used for purchasing tickets. It's important to store it in a way that the user doesn't have to take out her credit card and type it in every time. A user doesn't want pickpockets or purse snatchers in a rush hour station to get a look at her wallet. The choices are to store the number on the phone itself, perhaps encrypted, or store it on a central server, like Amazon does, and fetch it when she wants to purchase a ticket.

Which will users prefer? It might depend on when we ask them. If there had been a data breach in the last few weeks, like the one that hit Target in 2013, they'll want it stored on the handset. They'll figure a bad guy will focus on hitting big targets where he can steal millions at a time, not one at a time by stealing phones. There's not a whole lot you can do to prevent that. On the other hand, if Claire wants her monthly pass to automatically renew, she has to give the T some sort of ongoing financial authority, whether it's credit card or automatic checking account withdrawal. And once it's there, we might as well keep it all there.

With privacy, our biggest problem will be the tracking of user movements and locations. In theory, this information becomes a problem only when it is personally identifiable. We could give each user a unique identifier, a random number assigned when the app is installed. We would know that anonymous user 24168302 went into town on the 6:00 a.m. train and came home on the 4:30 p.m. train. We wouldn't know that particular user was Mary Smith, but we'd know somebody did it. We could then work out individual profiles, which could be of great use to data miners.

The problem is that if we collect this information, it's liable to get abused somewhere. We could, or someone could, correlate user movements with ticket purchases and work out who each user was.

Suppose the news leaked out that the T was collecting the movements of individual riders. "To serve you better," they'd doubtless say. "We're only doing good stuff with it." What do you suppose the local Fox News affiliate would do with that story? How long would it take for customers to ditch our app? That's like the dentist saying, "This won't hurt." No, it won't hurt *him* a bit, will it? Suppose one of the programmers got caught stalking an ex-girlfriend?

As riders, we don't have an intimate relationship with the T. We don't have any reason for them to be tracking us as individuals. I'd suggest that this app should not collect data on specific users, even if it's anonymized. If we're not recording it, we can't possibly leak it. Project managers will sleep a whole lot more soundly at night that way.

Step 7: Make It Just Work

Now that we've worked out our designs for this project, let's go back and review them against the commandments that I gave you in Chapter 7. We're trying make this app just work. How are we doing?

Start with Good Defaults

This is probably the biggest improvement that we've made from the original app. Instead of throwing all the documentation for the entire commuter rail network at the user, and forcing her to strain out the pieces she cares about, our app automatically deduces the pieces that she cares about. We generate her default stations from her ticket purchases, and her current location from cell-level positioning. We show them to her front and center.

Remember Everything That You Should

We do this very well in this app. The most important item that we remember is the user's usual commuting route—the stations that he goes to and from. We use that information to determine the schedules to show him, and the time to the next train.

Speak Your Users' Language

We are careful to speak our users' language at all times. Probably the biggest decision I made in relation to this was omitting the train number from the schedule grid view. Certainly the T uses train numbers internally, as airlines do. But riders, according to their interviews, never, ever think in terms of those. They always think in terms of the time: "Damn, missed the 6:20 and they canceled the 6:50; the next one goes at 7:14."

Don't Make Users Do Your Work

The original app made our users do a lot of work to find and then read the information they needed. This app automatically figures out what the user wants and then shows it to her. She's doing a whole lot less work than she used to do, as close as we can get to no work at all. Even the tabs that we show are carefully selected—the outbound trains if she's in town, the inbound trains if not. We've done this well.

Don't Let Edge Cases Dictate the Mainstream

The main case of the rail commuter is making the same trip over and over, day after day. This app is highly optimized for that case. If he wants something else, like "Hey, if I take the train in for the Bruins game on Saturday, when are the trains?" there's a link for it, but he'll have to do some work. A rail fan whose hobby is riding every line to every station will have to do much more work. We have carefully optimized for the main case.

Don't Make the User Think

This app's biggest de-thinker is the countdown timer. It shows the time until the next train, so you don't have to look at the schedule, look at the clock, and do math. It shows you the track number so you can go directly there. This app requires as little thinking as I could possibly make it.

Don't Confirm

We don't have any confirmation in this app. This app doesn't do anything that would require it.

Do Undo

The scheduling portion of the app doesn't have anything that we could undo. In the ticket purchase portion, perhaps we could allow return of purchased tickets. But the T doesn't refund paper tickets, so electronic tickets won't get refunded either.

Have the Correct Configurability

This app automatically detects the stations that the user travels to and from. If for some reason our automatic detection is wrong, or the user changes her pattern, we provide a link by which she can make changes. We also provide a link if she wants to look at other times. Nothing else is configurable. That's a good place to start for this app. We may gain a little more configurability in the future, such as the choice of putting the tabs at the top or bottom of the screen.

Lead the Witness

This app leads the witness in everything—automatically detecting which stations we use, which trains we ride, automatically showing us when the next one leaves. Compare it to the original app where the user has to dig for every last scrap. This is a damn good app, if I do say so myself. Which I do, because it is.

CHAPTER 9

CASE STUDY: MEDICAL PATIENT PORTAL

The field of medicine is the last major industry that the Internet has yet to penetrate. Almost all data interchange there still gets done with faxes. One young doctor told me, "My kids' babysitter makes better use of the Internet than we do here at [a major teaching hospital]."

Let's apply our newly learned UX skills and techniques to a Web portal for medical patients. We'll work through a case study for Boston's Beth Israel Deaconess Medical Center, which has such a thing. We can make it a whole lot better.

A Good First Try

Boston's Beth Israel Deaconess Medical Center, known locally as BI, has pioneered many advances in the medical arts. Its most popular is probably the "walking epidural," which relieves the pain of childbirth without immobilizing the patient. While BI doesn't have the world renown of some other hospitals, it scores well among those who know; both of my daughters were born there. People around here like to say that "Massachusetts General Hospital is the best hospital in the world. BI is the best hospital in Boston."

> note
>
> Beth Israel Hospital merged with Deaconess Hospital in 1996 to form Beth Israel Deaconess Medical Center. Cranky old-fart locals, among whom I number myself, continue to call it BI.

Another of BI's advances was its Internet portal for patients, www.patientsite.org. It was one of the world's first such portals, which you can deduce from the domain name they were able to snag. It allows patients to view test results, schedule appointments, request referrals or pre-scriptions, and send secure email to their physicians. It was built and hosted in-house by a team led by John Halamka, MD, and went live in 2000.

It was a very good first cut at that time. Dare I say valiant? The challenges that this team had to face—medical, legal, regulatory, political, managerial, and, oh yeah, technical—were and are huge (see, for example, www.ncbi.nlm.nih.gov/pmc/articles/PMC2274878/). The fact that it exists at all is a monumental accomplishment.

Nevertheless, examined from today's standards of usability, it needs a lot of work. Part of this is just age. Think how drastically everything else in the technological world has changed in the last 15 years. It should not surprise you that the usability trade-offs that were acceptable then no longer are. In this chapter we examine PatientSite's user experience today and make recommendations for upgrading it to the current standard of care. BI's PatientSite Web site was a pioneer. Applying our UX techniques to it can vault it into the forefront again.

Current State of the Art

We start using PatientSite at its entry page (Figure 9.1). Because of the confidentiality rules that apply to medical data, we have to log in every time. There is no option to stay logged in for a week, as Amazon allows. The entry screen layout is good. The picture is inviting. The text line explains to a new user what she can do with the site: "View your test results" (shown), "Make appointments," and so on. The picture and text change slowly enough that they're not disturb-ing. The login controls are standard, and the new-user registration link makes sense.

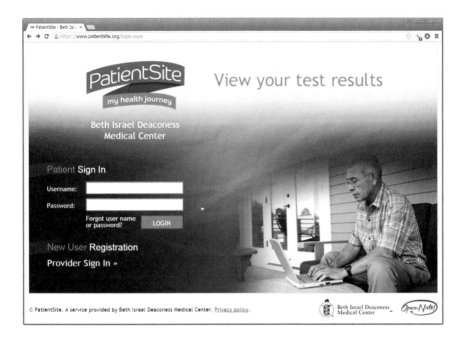

Figure 9.1   Beth Israel Deaconess Medical Center patient portal Web site.

Probably the only change needed would be to omit the separate login link for providers. I'd suggest accepting both patient and provider credentials on this screen and differentiating them internally as needed. Here the site is forcing the user to do the programmer's work, by selecting the correct login screen instead of having it done automatically based on the login ID. This particular instance is small, but we'll see this motif again throughout the site.

After logging in, we see the home screen, shown in Figure 9.2. As our upcoming analysis will explain, parts of it are good. Parts of it are OK but could be better with some additional work. And parts of it need to be completely rethought and redone.

Let's look at the good pieces first. The appointments schedule is at the top and center. The things that *you* have to do, the times and places when *you* have to be somewhere, are right in front of you when you first get to this page. That's good. Also, the links on the left side are obvious as the navigation structure. That's good too. We could argue about their groupings and some of their labels, but we'll let that slide for now.

What here is OK but needs some work? The appointment schedule at the top says, "Click for instructions." If we do that, we get the page shown in Figure 9.3, which shows us the department, location, best parking, and phone number. What if we don't know where the Shapiro Clinical Center or its garage is located? How about a link for a map or directions? They're common on most business or commercial sites today. There's a button to print the appointment

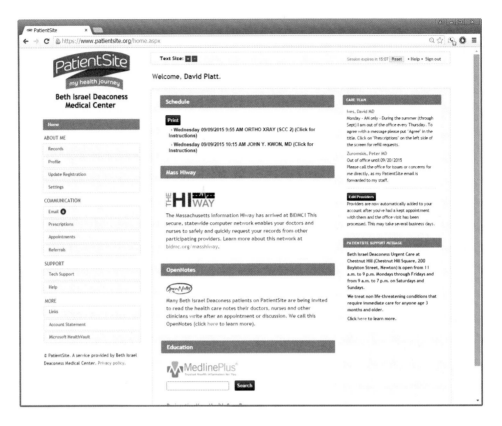

Figure 9.2   Beth Israel Deaconess Medical Center home page.

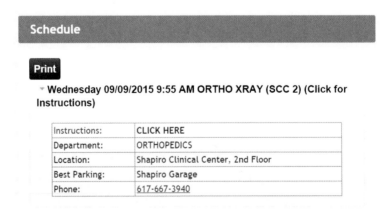

Figure 9.3   Appointment schedule after the first click. It invites you to click again.

details. How about a button for uploading them to our calendar so we can see them on our mobile devices? Again, this is common today on most sites that deal with schedules.

The biggest problem here is that it says , "Instructions: Click Here." Wait a minute, didn't we just do that? Did we have a brain fart and somehow forget? Aren't these the instructions we got from that clicking? (Yes, no, and yes.) If we click on this link, we get the page shown in Figure 9.4, which is indeed more instructions. If these are important, as they seem to be, they shouldn't be buried this deeply. What percentage of users actually click down deeply enough to see them? (Telemetry could tell us, but this Web site does not use telemetry to this level.) Or if they're not important, why distract us with them at all? Ideally we'd see the entire set of instructions with the first click, with the enhancements we just discussed.

Working our way down the home screen, the most valuable real estate on any Web site, we find the rest of it wasted. The Mass Hlway section, smack in the middle, is a description of a network that BI and other health care providers use to exchange data between hospitals. We don't need to see this every time we come in. We give PatientSite consent to use this on our behalf (separate screen, not shown), or not, and then never have to think about it again. Why is something that we never care about constantly consuming the most valuable real estate on the page? This is wrong.

The same applies to the OpenNotes section at the bottom center. This describes the system whereby you can see your doctor's note verbatim as soon as he places it in the system. This description has been here for at least several years, and as a user, I've never cared about it even once. Providing these notes is a good thing to do. But continually wasting this important space on the feature's description, as with Mass Hlway, is wrong.

For our final examination of PatientSite's current user experience, let's walk through the common case of viewing a patient's clinical data. This is one of the main reasons users come to

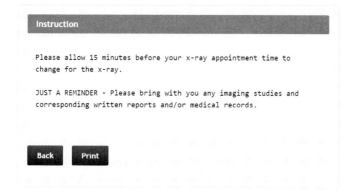

Figure 9.4 Instructions shown on the appointment schedule after the second click.

PatientSite. Its importance is shown by its placement (Records) as the first link in the navigation list. This was my experience:

I had a neurological test done at BI recently, and I wanted to view my results. Did I pass? Had I studied hard enough? Was my nose going to fall off or something? How would I find out about and then view my test results? The answer is: poorly. Let me show you.

I received an email on my regular email account. It said, "SignIn [sic] to PatientSite at https://www.patientsite.org to check the following messages: You have a new OpenNotes message(s)." It didn't tell me what sort of thing I had waiting for me. OK, I can see that, privacy regulations and all. Outside of PatientSite, all they're allowed to say is "We have something for you; please come get it." So I went to PS and logged in.

When I did, I saw exactly what you saw in Figure 9.2. There's no obvious entry point, no starting place at which to look for my new medical data, whatever it might be. I saw the Appointments window (at the time, empty) and descriptions of Mass HIway and OpenNotes, as wasteful then as now. Where's my new stuff? Those doctors stuck some needles in me a week ago, and the email told me to come here to see something new. But I saw no obvious indication of where it is or even what it is.

Maybe the email, the little red balloon with the 8? Could there be an email for me? Maybe. That's what brought me here, an email, and I don't see anything else it could be. Let me go look. Now I see the page shown in Figure 9.5. There's one message that says, "Your Note is

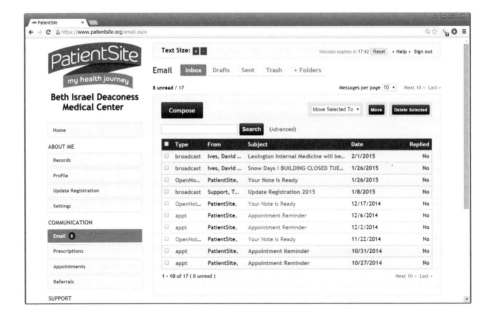

Figure 9.5   Secure email screen.

Ready," dated a week after the test. There is no mention of "the results of your neuro exam," or anything else that would tell me what each of these messages is about. Why not? Certainly it can't be security that forbids it; I'm already logged in to PatientSite. I can't imagine it's the ones that say "Appointment Reminder." The process of elimination suggests the one dated 12/17. Let me try that.

Ah, now I'm seeing an email message, as shown in Figure 9.6: "Dear Patient, We invite you to review the note . . ." It talks about an appointment or discussion. Well, I had a nasty test, involving needles, not an appointment or a discussion; and I had it on 12/09, not on 12/14, the date mentioned in the text, or on 12/17, the date of the email. Still, there's nothing else here that looks any better. I should probably look at what it tells me to look at.

How do I do that? "To read the note, please go to 'Records' on the left side of the PatientSite screen . . ." OK, I'll click on Records.

Whoa! Where did everybody go? My entire screen has changed, to a completely different layout and for no apparent reason (see Figure 9.7).

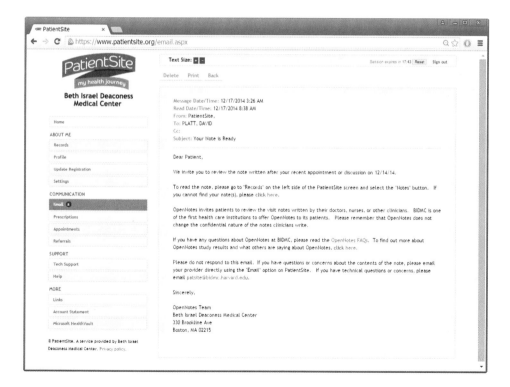

Figure 9.6   Confusing email telling me about a note after a recent appointment or discussion.

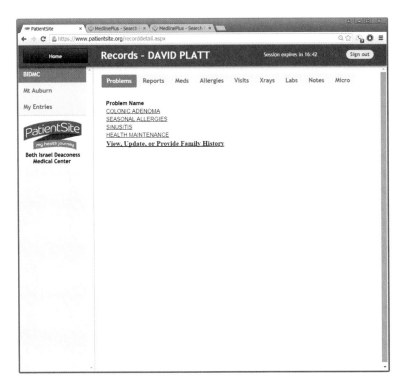

Figure 9.7   Beth Israel Deaconess Medical Center record viewing page.

What happened to my links down the left side? There are fewer of them now, and all their names have changed. BIDMC? OK, maybe, that's why I'm here. Mt. Auburn? That's a street near Harvard Square that I park on sometimes; what's it doing here? My Entries? I didn't make any entries. I want to see the results of my neuro test. Where did all those tabs on top come from? Problems? Sure, I've got problems, but I don't see anything here remotely dealing with my neuro test. How the hell can I get out of here? Try the Back button, I guess; that's what you do in a browser to go back, right?

Oops! Confirm Form Resubmission (Figure 9.8)? WTFFF?

What the hell? I didn't submit a form. I clicked on a link, didn't like where it took me, so I clicked Back. Now I'm in limbo. Confirm something? Confirm what? Something is seriously mafungoed. Maybe the Back button again? Ah, now I'm back to the page shown in Figure 9.5. Sheesh. Now what?

If there's one thing I learned in engineering school, it's "When all else fails, read the directions." OK, let's try that again. "To read the note, please go to 'Records' on the left side of the PatientSite screen and select the 'Notes' button." Wait. I have to remember two separate operations in my

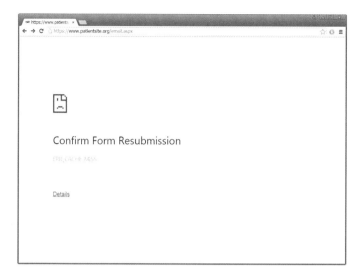

Figure 9.8 Confusing screen from hitting the Back button from another confusing screen.

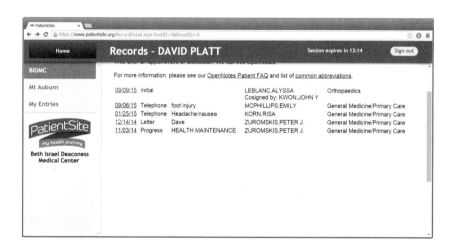

Figure 9.9 Confusing Notes screen.

head, and the instructions disappear after I do the first one? They can't just give me a link to the place I need to go? Or even an indication on the Records link that there's something new there for me? Again, we see the user doing work that the programmers should have done for her. If one of my UX students did this, I'd flunk her so fast she'd change her major to Sanskrit.

OK, here I am at the Notes screen (Figure 9.9). Letter? I didn't have a letter done; I had a nerve conduction study. Peter Zuromskis? He's my primary, but he's not the guy who did the test. He's a smart guy, he took the time to write me a letter, so I might as well have a look at what he has to say.

Figure 9.10   The medical record I came here to see.

I click on the letter from Peter Zuromskis, which is indeed about the test and does explain the medical technicalities in the way primary care physicians ought to do (Figure 9.10).

That was a whole lot more trouble, thinking and guessing and deducing, than it should have been.

PatientSite went live in 2000. That was also the year my first daughter was born—at BI. She will probably have her driver's license by the time you read this. That's a very long time in this industry.

The first users probably accessed PatientSite through dial-up modems (remember them?), some of them through AOL (remember it?). Windows 98 (you get the idea) was cutting edge. Existence, not ease of use, was the major goal of the PatientSite developers. Simply collecting this information and putting it in front of patients was a monumental accomplishment.

The patients were happy with it then because it beat the pants off what they previously had, which was nothing at all. They didn't mind having to do a tonsillectomy through the rectum to use the site. Learning how to do that was called "becoming computer literate." But the standard of care for user experience has risen astronomically. (One word: "iPhone.") Where BI once led, it now lags.

This evolution is similar to that of the automotive industry. The first automobile owners loved their Model T Fords, because having a car meant they could stop shoveling horse manure out of the barn every day. But it wasn't long before they took the Model T's basic functionality for granted and started demanding a better user experience: first with self-starters and heaters; then radios and automatic transmissions; today DVD, satnav, and multiple cup holders; tomorrow, independent self-driving.

The same progression is happening now across the software world. And nowhere is there more pent-up demand for a better UX than in the one-sixth of the US economy that comprises the medical industry. BI could be out on the cutting edge, with the careful application of the Plattski Protocol and not all that much coding.

Primary diagnosis: Outdated usability, due to rising standard of care.

Prescribed treatment: Full analysis and overhaul by contemporary UX standards.

Step 1: Who?

As always, we need to start with our users. Who are they?

The developers of the MBTA app in Chapter 8 had to deduce their user information from the advertisers' data, probably based on the T's own marketing studies, probably old and not all that detailed.

BI has exactly the opposite situation. BI has, by definition, an intimate relationship with every user who registers with PatientSite. BI knows their name and address, their age and gender, work and family situation, their insurance and related financial info. They have intimate medical information on all of their users, down to and including pictures of the inside of my colon. (See Figure 9 . . . nah, just kidding. But they do have it.) We can find out just about anything we want to know about our user population. A member of the PatientSite team said, "Our typical user is a middle-aged, college-educated, white female." So that's who we'll use for our first persona. And we'll create a second one, more speculative, to give us some notion about where PatientSite should be headed in the future.

Susan (Figure 9.11) was diagnosed with breast cancer about three months ago, at age 52. She lives in Natick, Massachusetts, with her husband, Bob. She works as a high school science teacher in the Natick public school system. She gets decent sick time through her union contract, but this cancer thing still sucks. Like many professional women nowadays, she delayed having kids until she felt herself established in life, so she has a son age 16 and a daughter age 14. Their golden retriever, Topsy, is 10 and starting to show her age as well.

Her cancer was somewhat advanced at the time of diagnosis, with three lymph nodes positive. Stage II is the technical term. She had surgery and is now undergoing chemotherapy. She will

Figure 9.11   Susan, a breast cancer patient who gets her care at BI. (Photo © iStock.com/nano)

have radiation when that's done. She is trying to keep on working through her chemotherapy, even though it's exhausting. She has many different appointments with different providers that she has to track. Some are at a suburban satellite clinic, which she prefers, but for others she has to drive into the main hospital in the Fenway section of Boston. She has a Red Sox schedule stuck to her refrigerator door so she knows when to schedule around the killer traffic that their games generate. She has lots of prescriptions to track: different chemo pills, various side effects medicines, and so on. She has physical therapy appointments for her arm as well.

She tracks all these on an older Dell laptop. Her son insisted that she get an iPhone, and she did, but she really hasn't mastered it yet and doesn't live on it the way he does. She borrows his iPad once in a while, though, taking it to her chemo infusions to read books and listen to music. She orders grocery deliveries on it via Peapod, one less chore she has to do in person.

It's always useful to create a secondary persona as well. Unless the user group is monolithic (hospital nurses, perhaps, or NFL players), it's good to have a second. So who should it be?

Let's not go older than Susan. While BI's patient population probably skews toward older people, one of the main reasons that computing hasn't caught on in the medical industry is that this population has the most difficulty using computers. They didn't grow up with them, they got them later in life, they don't trust them. The usage of computers in medicine likely won't break through to the mainstream until this population dies out and a more tech-savvy cohort moves in.

So the second persona needs to be younger. How about making this one male? For a little ethnic diversity, how about Asian? And why would he be talking to BI? When you look at statistics, you see chronic diseases entering the demographic pipeline today in younger and younger patient populations. These patients will consume ever-greater medical resources as they age and their chronic diseases turn acute. Information technology is often touted as the solution to this. So let's make him a type 2 pre-diabetic, to start examining how this kind of site would relate to a younger patient clientele (Figure 9.12).

Harry Chen is 30 years old. He came to Boston to study at MIT and never left. He works in Kendall Square, at a tech start-up so secret we can't even mention its name. He lives in Cambridge, Massachusetts.

His tech company health benefits include a complete physical once per year, and what do you know? Harry's blood chemistry screen came back pre-diabetic. Damn. Diabetes is a lifelong,

Figure 9.12 Harry, a young man with pre-diabetes, getting care from BI. (Photo © iStock.com/ DragonImages)

chronic thing. Harry really wants to head it off as much as possible. So he enrolled in Weight Watchers and exercise classes. He goes for quarterly blood work, to see what kind of progress he's making on it. His father died young of a heart attack, so Harry gets yearly EKGs as well.

Harry lives on his mobile phone, an iPhone 6s. If something isn't on his phone, it didn't happen, and he's not interested in it. A Windows PC is a boring thing that his parents used when they moved out to the suburbs and started taking commuter rail. All of his appointments are on his phone, his prescriptions, everything. If he needs anything in the medical realm (or any other, really), he expects to be able to tap a phone app and have it happen.

Step 2: What (and When, and Where, and Why)?

What problems do Susan and Harry need to solve, and what would they consider the characteristics of a good solution?

Modern medicine is a complicated thing, with many moving parts. Any sort of major illness, such as Susan has, or chronic illness, such as Harry is just starting to deal with, generates piles of data. The patients want to keep some sort of control over it, but it's increasingly convoluted. If we had to write their needs on a bumper sticker, it would say, "Tracking the intersection of my complex medical situation with the rest of my complex life." PatientSite is trying to smooth this out.

We'll express this thought in the form of stories so that the geeks who would code this app can understand what the users need. Here's what we come up with.

Story 1

Susan has a bad case of chemo brain and can't remember when her next appointment is. She wrote it down on her paper calendar, but she can't find that either. Fortunately, there's a desktop PC in her den which is too big and heavy for her to move and lose.

She turns on the PC and clicks the PatientSite icon that her son has thoughtfully placed on the desktop. The browser remembers her user ID and password, so she doesn't have to waste time typing them in. (They're written on a sticky note stuck to the monitor in case the browser forgets.)

Susan finds the section for appointments and looks at her collection, scanning for where and when they are. Let's see, the next one is this Saturday. That's the problem with wanting to keep on working through chemo: her weekends get eaten. Her Red Sox schedule shows home games on both days this weekend, so she hopes she doesn't have to drive in to the main BI campus.

Ah, her appointment's in the suburban office, early on Saturday. Great! Well, sort of. It's still a chemo appointment. But at least she doesn't have Red Sox game-day traffic on top of it.

She writes it down on a sticky note (the pad is taped to the monitor, the pen attached with a string, so they can't disappear). She sticks it on the back of her hand to remind her to ask her husband or son to give her a ride. She wishes there were an easier way but doesn't have the energy to explore one.

Story 2

Susan is having dose-dense chemotherapy for her Stage II breast cancer. This means that she gets the usual dosage of chemotherapy for her condition, but with less time between infusions than was previously allowed. The statistical survival advantage is small but definite. And she figures she might as well get this chemo crap over with sooner anyway.

Because her recovery time between chemo infusions is shorter, Susan is given medications to help boost her blood count. Her doctors need to monitor how well these are working, partly to plan her chemo and partly to make sure she doesn't get sick from something else. If she has to be readmitted to the hospital now, the medical practice that cares for her will incur financial penalties from the insurers. So they have her come to the lab and get blood drawn twice in the two-week break between chemo infusions.

Susan wants to keep an eye on her blood work to know how she's doing. In fact, she's obsessed with it. Perhaps it's her attempt to maintain some control, or at least the illusion of control, over her treatment process and hence her disease. Every time she gets blood work done, she checks the Web site hourly until she sees the results posted. She can't bear to wait for the email notification, as it often doesn't arrive until several hours after the lab results become available, and sometimes it doesn't arrive at all.

She finishes dinner (not a whole lot of appetite) and sits down to watch some TV. Before she turns it on, she wants to check if her blood results are in from that afternoon. Where's that damn iPad? Oh, yeah, right here between the couch cushions. How's the charge? Good enough. She launches the Safari browser, brings up PatientSite, logs in with the saved ID and password. There are her current blood work results. Are they good? The red color indicates counts outside normal limits. Hmm, what were her numbers during her last chemo cycle? She takes a look at those. Actually today's numbers look OK; she's ahead of the last cycle by a point or two. She puts down the iPad, wishing this damn thing were over.

Thinking about her disease leads inevitably to thoughts of her own mortality. She decides she doesn't want to watch the Red Sox tonight, especially because they stink this year. A hot bath, a stiff drink, and a good book sound a whole lot better. She puts down the iPad, pours a glass, and heads upstairs. She wonders if Topsy will outlive her.

Story 3

Harry was diagnosed with pre-diabetes at his initial physical. That doesn't surprise his doctor one bit. The incidence of pre-diabetes is on the rise in younger adults.

If all of today's pre-diabetic young adults progress to full diabetes at historic rates, the resultant medical need would collapse all of civilization. In an attempt to proactively manage pre-diabetes to arrest (or at least slow) this progression, Beth Israel is running a study using lower-cost health coaches. Harry is enrolled in this study and has been randomized into the higher-intervention arm.

To manage his care, and to see what's working and what isn't, BI has to collect a lot of data about Harry on an ongoing basis. They'll get this data only if it doesn't require much effort on Harry's part. The ideal amount of effort is nothing at all; the second choice is nothing he's not already doing.

Harry is given a bathroom scale connected to the Internet and told to stand on it every time he gets out of the shower. That sends his weight to BI's database. His exercise, both from day-to-day activities and also at the gym, is automatically entered by his Apple Watch. The most difficult part for Harry is entering everything he eats, using a separate smartphone app such as SparkPeople. Harry doesn't mind this too much, as he lives on his phone anyway and usually has it in hand when he sits down to eat. It gives him a chance to show off his new iPhone 6s and have people admire it.

Every week, Harry has a 15-minute video conversation with his health coach. (This is in direct contrast to longer, less frequent sessions, which is the main innovation being tested in this study.) Harry would never touch a PC-based Web browser unless someone held a gun to his head. So this session is done via a custom-developed mobile app on his phone. The coach reviews what he's eaten in the last week and the amount of exercise he's gotten. She suggests changes that he could make. After a year of this, they'll compare how well he's done with the progress of other patients. Maybe they can keep him healthier longer.

Step 3: How?

The biggest problem that we saw on PatientSite is that the user's clinical information is very hard to find and read. There's no obvious starting point, and it's organized confusingly and displayed poorly once we do find it. The appointments are not bad but could be better.

We need to redesign the home page to make it do what home pages are supposed to do: provide immediate display of the most important data, with a logical navigation structure providing access to the rest. I sat down with Balsamiq to start working it out.

Because the user's highest priorities are clinical information and appointments, I decided that these should live on the home page. The first mockup I did is shown in Figure 9.13. The center column contains the clinical information relating to the logged-in patient. There is a separate entry for each encounter the patient has with the medical system, displayed in chronological order. Any user who has used Facebook or an email program will find this timeline layout familiar. Because it extends, conceptually, back to the beginning of the patient's relationship with BI, we'll dedicate the entire center column to it.

Each encounter displays a summary so the user can decide if she wants to open it for more information. In the figure, we see from the summaries that the patient has most recently had blood work done. A few days before that, she had a chemo infusion, preceded by pre-chemo blood work, preceded by a call to her primary physician for nausea. Each encounter has a link that opens to show more details, which I'll show in a later example. It's conceptually similar to the layout of messages in an email program.

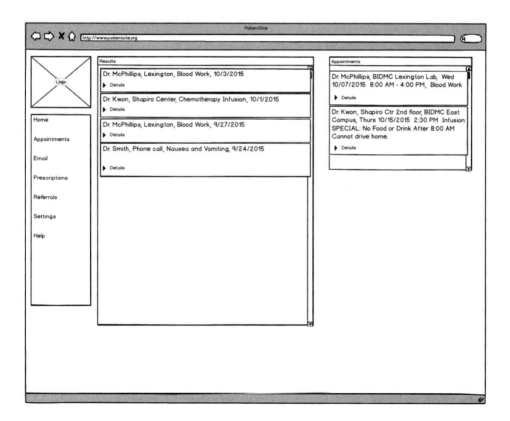

Figure 9.13 First draft, the basic layout of the new PS home page.

I've moved the appointment box to the top right of the screen, because it has fewer entries in it. At any given time, a user might have two, three, maybe four appointments scheduled. But the appointments disappear as they slip into the past, while the encounter list just gets longer.

If the screen gets narrow, either from a PC with a small monitor or a tablet in portrait orientation, the site will automatically adjust itself to a single column, with the Appointments window on top and the Results window below (not shown). If it ever gets really tiny, as with a phone, we might switch to a tabbed arrangement (not shown either).

Here's how I now present the clinical data: Each encounter displays its basic data in the small block—who, when, where, and what. If the user clicks the Details arrow, it opens up, showing the details of the encounter, as shown in Figure 9.14. Any additional work that was done in this encounter is shown; in this case prescriptions, but also possibly X-rays or labs, are shown with a link.

When Susan finds her most recent lab results at the top of the center column, she clicks on the Details arrow to open it, and there is a link to the tests she's had. When she clicks on that link, she sees the results in a popup balloon. If she wants further details, or an explanation of their meanings, there's a link for that. But with her ongoing treatment, Susan knows what these mean (Figure 9.15).

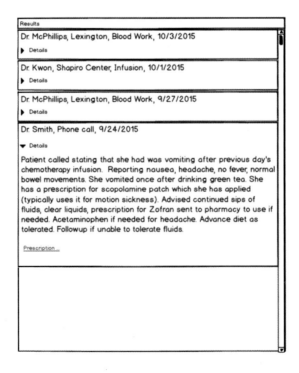

Figure 9.14   Close-up of the Results section, encounter expansion.

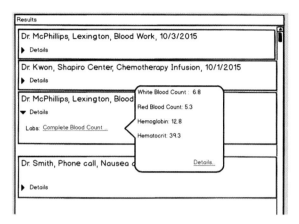

Figure 9.15 Close-up of the Results section, displaying lab results.

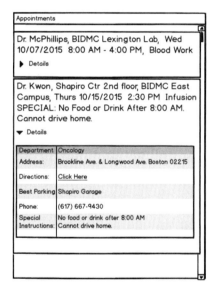

Figure 9.16 Close-up of the Appointments section, showing appointment expansion.

Moving now to the Appointments window, we show the soonest first, moving later in time as you scroll down the window. Each appointment box contains the information that an experienced user needs to know—when, where, and with whom. If a user has been to this location before, as Susan has, that's all he'll need, and he won't click on the Details link. He can click on the Details arrow to get the rest of the information if he's new (Figure 9.16).

Note that I didn't use the space at the lower right corner of the home page, under the Appointments window. I'll leave it open for further developments.

Step 4: Try It Out

As always, the first mockup isn't intended to be final, or even all that good. It represents a straw man that we can start poking at. I tried these mockups on several users and potential users. I took one shortcut here: a former student named Aimee works in tech support at a medical practice, helping users try to use this kind of system from a commercial vendor. She knows a lot about what kinds of choices they are offered, which ones work, and which ones cause trouble. I tried some other users who fit the demographic: middle-aged college-educated white females, some who are cancer patients and some not. I did some role-playing exercises with my students and teaching assistants, asking them to behave in character. And to wrap things up, I had a good long talk with the surviving husband of the late woman after whom I patterned the Susan persona.

Every user liked the clinical data being right out front. The ones who had seen PatientSite before loved the fact that they no longer had to go digging for things. They liked the timeline arrangement. They liked the careful consideration of the different types of users who view the Appointments window—the experienced users, who need only date and time and place reminder, and the newbies, who need to click for directions and parking.

And then, of course, after they say they like this and they like that, comes the giant *"Buuut . . ."* That's good. As I said in Chapter 3, you need to understand that this is a necessary and desirable part of the process. It is sometimes hard not to take things personally, but the process is very much unfolding as it should. The users are not attacking us personally. They're developing and enhancing our ideas, sometimes coming up with better ones. We must try very hard to say, "Mmm, yes, thank you, that's quite interesting, tell me more. What would be good for you, do you think?" rather than "No, dummy, it's right over there, can't you see it?"

The first thing my test users wanted was for more results to be shown in the encounter stream without having to click again. For example, why should they have to click on the Prescription link (in Figure 9.14) to see what the medication and dosage should be? They were viewing the encounter, and the prescription is part of it; why not just show at least a summary of that data? You could have a link to the full thing if you wanted. I explored that with the mockup in Figure 9.17. After showing them this new option, they said they liked it better.

A patient like Susan who is getting repeated tests wants to compare her current results to her previous results. Is she ahead of or behind last time? Does it look good enough for her to get her chemo next week? Is her white count high enough to teach school, where those little monsters boil up a cauldron of infection?

As always, any sort of comparison needs to be easy to use and require very little thinking on the part of the user. Susan does not need or want the ability to select any arbitrary interval for comparison. So I mocked up an automatic graphic display. This way she'll be able to open the encounter and see what tests she's had. If she clicks on the item, a graphical window displays it plotted over time (Figure 9.18). It's automatically scaled in horizontal and vertical so that it makes sense. The test users loved this as well.

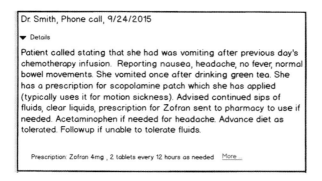

Figure 9.17 Prescription detail automatically shown.

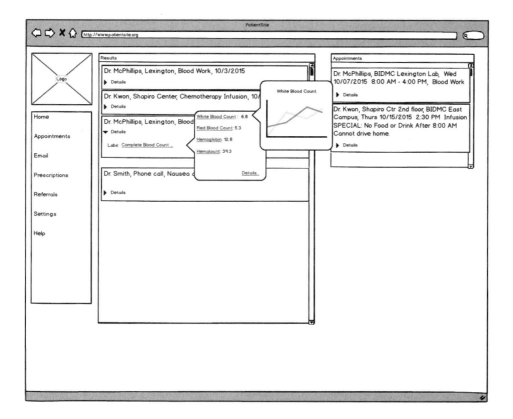

Figure 9.18 Automatic graphing of a selected lab value.

Looking at the appointment screen, the one thing that every single test user asked for was getting the scheduled appointments into their online calendars so they could view them in their mobile devices. That isn't something that the developers of PatientSite thought about at its inception. The first iPhone didn't come out until 2007, roughly half of PatientSite's current lifetime, and the mobile sector didn't become ubiquitous for about two or three years after that. But Boston is one of the techiest towns in the world; calendar sync should become possible sooner rather than later. Until I know how to get it done, I'll provisionally put a Sync to Calendar button next to the Print button (not shown).

Sometimes users make appointments through PatientSite, and sometimes they make them through other channels. For example, as Susan is finishing one appointment, the doctor will often say something like "Make an appointment to come back in four weeks." Susan will usually do that at the office desk before she leaves, while she's thinking about it and has the most choices available. Those appointments appear magically in PatientSite, as they should. Susan would also like them to be sent magically to her online calendar.

As I worked with different users, I found different desires for reminders. Reducing no-shows is critical for BI from a business standpoint. The hospital already employs several channels of reminders, such as snail mail and telephone voice messages (and a cumbersome email system, described later in the discussion of security and privacy). This could easily be extended to text messaging as well. And if the app will put appointments into online calendars, which platforms should it support? Microsoft Outlook, Google+, or Apple iCalendar? Very good question.

As we worked on one major need, the information architecture redesign, we stumbled onto this other need, calendar sync and reminders, that wasn't obvious at the beginning. This is not unusual. That's what this rapid iteration of low-fidelity mockups leads to. We don't have time to work calendars or reminders into the current development sprint, as I don't have time to work it into this chapter. It needs to become a separate story—possibly as part of Susan's intake appointment after her diagnosis. But the earlier we find it, the more chance we have of working it into the project sooner. We'll make note of it and put it aside for the next iteration.

Finally, one patient raised the notion that we might want to examine our encounters in ways other than chronologically. For example, we might want to see all our surgeries, or our X-rays, or encounters with Dr. Smith. How could we do this?

Email programs generally provide the capability of sorting messages by standard fields—by date or by sender, occasionally by topic or presence of an attachment, rarely by anything else. Medical messages are more complex. We could have a huge search screen, with advanced options (Doctor = "Smith" and EncounterType = "X-Ray" + BodyPart = "Left Foot," etc.). The user would have to do a whole lot of thinking to accomplish the simplest things.

It seems that the simplest searches are the best. Again, email programs usually allow for searches—"Find me all the occurrences of 'carpool,' or 'flogging.'" We could very easily

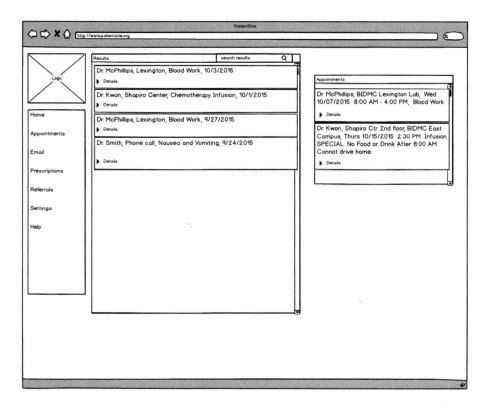

Figure 9.19 Search box in the upper right corner for messages.

implement this on PatientSite: "Find me all my encounters containing occurrences of 'appendix' or 'penicillin.'" Want things written by Dr. Smith? Type in "Smith." Want X-rays and Dr. Smith? Type in "X-ray Smith" or "Smith X-ray." It's conceptually just like a Google search. We could include a simple search box, as shown in Figure 9.19. Here it is in the upper right corner of the Results window title bar, to indicate that Results are what the search applies to. It's similar to the email search feature in Microsoft Outlook. We might as well start there. We'd have to experiment with that placement. Its success would depend on how often users actually used it.

It would really be great to make this search function as good as Google's. Recall discussions in this book about Google's auto-suggest and auto-fetch features. Imagine that our app had a search field for the encounter chain. Suppose a user wanted to see all her X-ray results. She would start typing "X." The search box would, as does Google, suggest what most users type after starting with X, which could only be "-ray." And while it does that, it would pre-fetch the records that conform to that field which have any mention of X-ray in them. This would be an absolute killer feature. The only question is whether BI's developers could actually implement it, cost-effectively, with their relatively low unit volume. Perhaps, as a nonprofit, they could get Google to sponsor it and give them the code or something.

A Quick Speculation: Health Coach Mobile App

We wanted to start taking a look at the future of online health care, so we came up with Harry. Here he is, 30 years old, pre-diabetic. It would be good to change his lifestyle and habits now. But that's a very hard thing for anyone to do. After the initial panic of his diagnosis, Harry feels fine. Any future problems are abstract and far away. He swore he'd be good, but eating food he doesn't like and working out (which he doesn't like either) are regimens that are very hard to stick to. How can we help shape Harry's choices today?

We can get him to put an app on his phone. This will allow his health coach to communicate with him, ideally to guide him into the paths of righteousness. It looks like Figure 9.20.

When I showed this mockup to students matching Harry's age and style, I encountered a curious dichotomy. Half of the students thought that a video conversation with his health coach would produce the best results. When we have a direct connection to a human being, the patient might try to please that human, or at least not disappoint her. All of the older students were in this half.

On the other hand, some, but not all, of the younger students felt that text messaging was a better means of communication. If you have to set up a meeting, both people have to be

Figure 9.20   A video version of the health coach app for Harry. More research is needed.

Figure 9.21   A text message version of the health coach app for Harry.

available at the same time, which is always tricky. But if the coach just sends texts ("Harry, your GPS shows you at Dunkin' Donuts! You better be telling me it's just for a friend." "No, it's just a black coffee, honest! The line was too long at Starbucks."), they don't have to be available at the same time. You'll get a better response this way, says the group. Figure 9.21 shows this approach.

We agreed that more research is needed. And that's exactly the sort of thing that they do at BI. I leave this idea confidently in their hands. Perhaps set goals and targets? Perhaps show him percentiles, maybe prizes? We are probably going to be breaking ground with this new study, and it will lead to several research papers.

Step 5: Telemetry Plan

Compared to the MBTA example in the previous chapter, PatientSite has a lot more moving parts. It's especially important to measure exactly what our users are doing so that we can optimize their experiences.

By looking at the extensions of its pages (.aspx), we can deduce that PS is mostly written in Microsoft .NET and therefore is hosted on Microsoft Internet Information Server. Our first line of telemetry, therefore, will be looking at the page logs that this program produces. They'll tell us how often each page gets served up.

Just this one simple data set will tell us a lot. Which pages are shown most often? After it's served up, how many times is each page submitted, as opposed to being canceled? For example, if Referrals is served 100 times, but submitted only ten times, perhaps users aren't getting value from it. Maybe they're confused when they see it. How often do they use PatientSite to make appointments? How about to refill prescriptions, which users can easily do through other channels such as their pharmacy's phone line?

Because users have to log in to PatientSite before they can accomplish anything, we know exactly who uses the system, exactly when, and exactly what they do. It would be interesting to create a histogram of usage profiles: The top 10% of users are responsible for 50% of the logins and 80% of the hits, or whatever. The bottom 50% of users account for only 10% of usage. Perhaps 33% of users create an account and then never touch it again. What could be done to maintain their interest? (A better UX, obviously.) Maybe we'd divide the users into three groups—heavy, moderate, and light—and monitor their usage patterns accordingly. We should also get some notion as to how long patients spend on their PatientSite sessions.

Now that we've improved the site's usability, we can measure how well its components are working. For example, how far down the timeline do users typically scroll? How often does a user scroll back by a month? Six months? Longer? The answers are most likely: once in a while, hardly ever, and never. How often is an appointment expanded to show its details?

In the MBTA example, we avoided collecting information too intimately. The relationship between users and the MBTA is casual at best, and we didn't want the app to get too close. ("What? A different station on Monday? You must have been at your mistress's house." And so on.) Users don't trust the MBTA all that much, don't want to, and shouldn't be asked to.

But a user's relationship with her medical providers is as intimate as it gets. She expects BI to collect and store her medical data so that they can provide the best care. Eyeglass prescription? Check. Blood type? You bet. Date of last period? When it's relevant, sure. And so on. She would get angry if they didn't have what she needed, if she got hurt because they couldn't find some piece of data that they should have known.

A research institution such as BI is constantly looking for new ways to slice and dice data. And PatientSite provides them with an incredible amount of data for mining. Learning things from sifting the pile of data that they already have is a whole lot faster and cheaper than enrolling live patients in a clinical test. And data mining is much easier to get through the ethics committees that have to approve any sort of study, because it doesn't involve changing any patient's treatment; it's just looking at what was done for patients and comparing outcomes.

We could expect to see all kinds of studies done on PatientSite's data. For example, what types of drugs are most commonly refilled? Does it vary by the patient's primary diagnosis? Does it have any relation to future addiction problems? Which appointments are most commonly rescheduled? And so on. The data is there. Someone will figure out something good to do with it. BI is a research institution. That's what they do. Maybe they'll figure out another walking epidural from it.

Plan on recording everything that you can, and then plan on slicing and dicing it in ways you never imagined. And plan on getting frequent requests to measure new things.

Step 6: Security and Privacy Plan

Medical data, such as this site handles, is about the most confidential thing you will ever deal with. Geeks who transition into the medical industry from other industries may not completely get this. They'll wonder, "Hey, how much do I really care if someone finds out I have a wart on my big toe?" But, for example, nobody wants their spouse to find out about the dose of syphilis they brought back from Las Vegas. There's no good way to tell which pieces are confidential, so you have to treat everything that way. It's not a new problem: the original Hippocratic Oath, approximately 2,500 years old, contains references to confidentiality. And so it is, must be, with our programs that deal with such.

The law recognizes the need for confidentiality, placing medical data under some of the most restrictive, almost brutal, regulations. The primary law is called HIPAA, pronounced "HIP-uh." It was passed in 1996 and thus predates essentially everything in today's technological world. While HIPAA pays plenty of attention to locking things down, there's not a whole lot of thought given to the opportunity cost when you can't get to something that you need, or the users' hassle budget and its inevitable workarounds. Go back and read Chapter 6 about security, and understand that the people who structured the regulations weren't thinking that way.

So: what sort of security and privacy does PatientSite enforce? Because of the confidentiality of the information, it's more like what a bank does and less like what Amazon does. First, you can't see anything at all until you log in (unlike Amazon, which shows your most recent purchases). Your password needs to conform to HIPAA regulations (at least eight characters, at least one letter and one number, and either a special character or a mix of upper and lower cases). They do not require you to change it (which saves me a rant here). PatientSite will log you out after you have been quiescent for 18 minutes, giving you a warning when you are getting close. It does not give you an option to stay logged in.

What is the user's hassle budget, and what kinds of workarounds will he use when it is exceeded? Users who log in to PatientSite frequently will want to have their credentials remembered somehow so they don't have to type them in every time. Informed, diligent users will employ some sort of password manager, such as Norton Identity Safe, to accomplish this. The lazy masses, containing almost everyone in the world including myself, will simply have their Web browser remember the user ID and password, as they do for most other sites.

As always, the users' hassle budgets depend on how easy it is to accomplish their goals in some other way. We can request a prescription refill at PatientSite if we want to. But if we've filled it at Walmart, we can dial the phone number on the label, key in the prescription number, and press 5 for a refill. If we have no more refills on the prescription, Walmart will automatically fax our doctor to request a new prescription. Is PatientSite easier or harder than this? It depends on whether we're more a phone kind of person or a PC kind of person. If we have the pill bottle in our hand, we aren't going to turn on our PC, bring up PatientSite, and do it there. On the other hand, if we're already in PatientSite for something else, we'll probably use PatientSite for the refill.

When PatientSite has something new to tell a patient, it sends an ordinary email to our regular email account. Because of the need for confidentiality, this email contains very little information: "Hello, there's something new here for you; please come look at it." Sometimes the information, when we log in and view it, is indeed confidential and deserves this treatment. But often it isn't, and the login is wasted effort. Looking at my current PatientSite email, only eight of the 24 messages currently in it fall under this category, and I'm including tech support responses in those eight.

The rest should have been sent to my open account, saving me the trouble of logging in to get them. These include five appointment reminder messages. They currently tell me that I have an upcoming appointment, and I need to log in to see the details. I would find it much more convenient if the original open email contained the relevant information: "You have an upcoming appointment at 11:00 on Thursday with Dr. Kwon on the 2nd floor of the Shapiro Center." HIPAA seems to say that this is allowed. My dentist leaves such detailed messages on my phone answering machine, and also in the email and text message reminders that she sends me. So does another non-BI medical practice I sometimes use. Why not PatientSite on my email (and text messages, if we ever get there)?

The other 11 of 24, almost half of my emails from BI, contain public information that has been misclassified: the hours of an upcoming flu clinic, or a notice that the building is closed today because of snow. These are not confidential at all. They could have been published in any newspaper. There's no reason for users to have to log in through their secure channel to see these.

One user reports that "when I get a message that I'm not expecting, then I have to log in and see if it's something I really care about it. Usually it isn't. But since it comes from my doctor, I can't just let it go." Almost two-thirds of my messages fall into this category. PatientSite could do a better job than this.

PatientSite does not attempt to handle the case of one user accessing another user's data. For example, my health insurance company's Web site allows me to see data on myself and my minor children, but not my wife's unless she grants me access through a permission process. In PS, one account is one patient, and nobody can see anyone else's. In this case, the users' workaround is simply to give their credentials to the party they want to look at them: an older patient to an adult child, or one spouse to another, or a minor to a parent. It's probably a good call on PatientSite's part, as the correct implementation would be difficult, and the current workaround is easy.

Step 7: Make It Just Work

We've done a lot of good work improving this site. Let's go back and review our improvements against the commandments that I gave you in Chapter 7. How can we make this Web site just work?

Start with Good Defaults

PatientSite's original layout had one very good default strategy: automatically presenting the user's appointments top and center. Our new design enhances the default home page by automatically showing a user's clinical records as well, most recent first.

Remember Everything That You Should

I didn't really address this issue as I worked my way through the overhaul. I wouldn't bother remembering items such as exactly where the user had scrolled in the clinical data. I'd definitely remember the text size setting, though, if the user chose one.

Speak Your Users' Language

Medicine is a field of incredibly vast and rich terminology. Even its practitioners commonly make mistakes in it. For example, my own records on PatientSite contain an instance in which a radiologist wrote about my metacarpal (hand) bone, when he was clearly looking at my metatarsal (foot) bone. We need to be careful not to add another layer of confusing nomenclature for dealing with the site. Putting all of our clinical data in one section, front and center, instead of requiring our users to search, is helpful. Also helpful would be an overhaul of the navigation links—what's the difference between Profile and Settings? We'll add this to the backlog for our next iteration.

Don't Make Users Do Your Work

The default presentation of the user's clinical records greatly decreases the amount of navigating that the user has to do. Our search capability on the clinical records decreases it even more. We have greatly decreased the amount of work a user has to do.

Don't Let Edge Cases Dictate the Mainstream

We've moved the mainstream case of viewing clinical data to the front and center. The edge cases no longer affect it. Good job there.

Don't Make the User Think

Having to search around for my clinical data required a whole lot of poking and thinking and deducing. For seeing new clinical records, we've reduced the work to zero. For seeing older ones, we've reduced it to a simple scroll, and for seeing specific content, we've provided a search capability similar to many apps that users are familiar with. We've lowered the amount of thinking to a bare minimum. Good job there too.

Don't Confirm

The parts of this site that we've examined don't have any confirmation dialogs. That's as it should be. We'll be sure to keep it that way as we continue our overhaul.

Do Undo

The parts of this site that we've examined don't perform any actions that might need to be undone. We'll keep this in mind as we continue our overhaul.

Have the Correct Configurability

The parts of this site that we examined don't have any sort of configurability, and I don't see the need for any. The site does contain some configurability options, accessed via the Settings, Profile, and Update Registration links. We'll look into configuration in our next iteration, probably starting with our overhaul of the notification system.

Lead the Witness

This site will greatly benefit by leading the witness in the search term field. I'd love to pre-fetch the data as Google does, but I wouldn't be surprised if this was beyond the system's capability. There is, however, no excuse today for not at least providing auto-suggestion as the user types.

It wouldn't take that long or cost that much to make this a killer site again.

INDEX

REGISTER YOUR PRODUCT at informit.com/register

Access Additional Benefits and SAVE 35% on Your Next Purchase

- Download available product updates.

- Access bonus material when applicable.

- Receive exclusive offers on new editions and related products.
  (Just check the box to hear from us when setting up your account.)

- Get a coupon for 35% for your next purchase, valid for 30 days. Your code will
  be available in your InformIT cart. (You will also find it in the Manage Codes
  section of your account page.)

Registration benefits vary by product. Benefits will be listed on your account page
under Registered Products.

InformIT.com–The Trusted Technology Learning Source
InformIT is the online home of information technology brands at Pearson, the world's foremost
education company. At InformIT.com you can

- Shop our books, eBooks, software, and video training.
- Take advantage of our special offers and promotions (informit.com/promotions).
- Sign up for special offers and content newsletters (informit.com/newsletters).
- Read free articles and blogs by information technology experts.
- Access thousands of free chapters and video lessons.

Connect with InformIT–Visit informit.com/community
Learn about InformIT community events and programs.

informIT.com
the trusted technology learning source

Addison-Wesley • Cisco Press • IBM Press • Microsoft Press • Pearson IT Certification • Prentice Hall • Que • Sams • VMware Press

ALWAYS LEARNING   PEARSON